THE COLLECTOR'S GUIDE TO

HARKER

POTTERY

Identification and Value Guide

U.S.A.

By Neva Colbert

COLLECTOR BOOKS

A Division of Schroeder Publishing Co., Inc.

The current values in this book should be used only as a guide. They are not intended to set prices, which vary from one section of the country to another. Auction prices as well as dealer prices vary greatly and are affected by condition as well as demand. Neither the Author nor the Publisher assumes responsibility for any losses that might be incurred as a result of consulting this guide.

Searching For A Publisher?

We are always looking for knowledgeable people considered to be experts within their fields. If you feel that there is a real need for a book on your collectible subject and have a large comprehensive collection, contact us.

COLLECTOR BOOKS
P.O. Box 3009
Paducah, Kentucky 42002-3009

Additional copies of this book may be ordered from:

COLLECTOR BOOKS
P.O. Box 3009
Paducah, Kentucky 42002-3009

@$17.95. Add $2.00 for postage and handling.

Copyright: Neva W. Colbert, 1993

Printed by IMAGE GRAPHICS, INC., Paducah, Kentucky

—Dedication—

To Momma. . . who taught me to love "Nice Things."
To Chuck. . . who taught me to love pottery.
To Paul. . . who taught me about Harker.
To Don. . . who taught me about love.

– Acknowledgments –

Soon after I started to work on this book, I began to refer to it as "the book" rather than "my book," because I realized that I could no longer claim sole responsibility for the labor. An undertaking like this is not a solo effort, and I want to thank those who helped.

My husband, Don, was my fellow researcher, chief critic, photographer and my greatest support. Paul Pinney searched his memory and his basement for information and examples. Valma Baxter graciously lent us her photos, her expertise, and her memories. Fellow collector Beverly Thompson encouraged me to write this book. Joan Wirr shared her genealogical research on the Harker and Boyce families. Kelly Namey guided two amateurs through the confusing process of photography.

Nancy Sabo of Nancy's Antiques in Pleasant Grove, Ohio, one of many dealers who went out of their way to help us, shared her knowledge of antiques and items from her collection of Harker ware.

Donna Juszczak, Carol Chaffee, Phil Rickerd, and Mark Twyford of the Ohio Historical Society Museum of Ceramics went beyond the call of duty to give us every help available. The staffs of the public library of Chester, West Virginia and those of St. Clairsville, East Liverpool, and Zanesville, Ohio, as well as the Ohio Inter-Library Loan System, made research infinitely easier.

Our daughters — Cathy, Carla, and Corinne — shared their collections, going for months without sugar bowls, as Kelly, Don, and I struggled with the photography, and they enjoyed correcting their English-teacher/mother's prose. Good friend and fellow teacher, Mary Harley, spent hours proofreading word by word to keep me from embarrassing myself in print.

And lastly I want to thank those who paved the way for my research, especially Jo Cunningham, whose *Collector's Encyclopedia of American Dinnerware* inspired this book and who graciously took time to advise a novice. *The City of Hills and Kilns* by William C. Gates Jr. made the world and work of the early potters come alive. *The East Liverpool, Ohio, Pottery District: Identification of Manufacturers and Marks* by Gates and Dana E. Ormerod was invaluable in solving many problems. I must also thank Lois Lehner, who writes with both wit and wisdom about American dinnerware. I owe a big debt to these and others who loved pottery enough to learn about it and to share their research with all collectors.

I want to add a word about my research and scholarship for those who will find my errors. First of all, I did not use standard page and source citations because I felt that they would slow down the flow of the book. I wanted this to be a conversation with fellow collectors, not a lecture. I have included a bibliography, and I have given credit to all quotations and conclusions. Secondly, I deliberately chose to refer to Harker Pottery and other potteries as "they" rather than the grammatically correct "it" because to me the potters themselves are the soul of the factory. I have a framed photograph of the Harker work force, including my father-in-law Charles Colbert, my friends Paul Pinney and Valma Baxter, and many others. They were Harker Pottery.

—Table of Contents—

Introduction

The first time that I saw someone check the bottom of a cup, I thought, "This man is very nervous or very weird." It was our first date, so I hoped that he was merely nervous and asked why he was inspecting the china. He explained that because he came from a family of potters and lived in a town dominated by potteries, he was curious about the origin of the dishes. "Shenango," he pronounced, as if that settled everything.

In a way, it did. As the child of generations of craftspeople — seamstresses who inspected the insides of garments, a telephone lineman who watched the wire overhead rather than the scenery as he drove, a stogie maker who still enjoyed the fragrance and shape of a good cigar long after he abandoned the trade and the habit — I understood professional curiosity and pride. So, I accepted my date's behavior as normal, but I didn't copy it. However, I did marry him.

Many years, three children, and several sets of broken dishes later, I saw a plate on a flea market table that looked familiar. When I turned it over and saw the Harker mark, I remembered clearly my father-in-law's face and voice as he proudly showed me the process by which that plate had been made. I thought of the lovely little dish and cup sets that he had made our two older daughters before he retired and Harker Pottery closed. So I bought the plate for fifty cents and told my husband, Don, that I was buying it for our youngest daughter, Corinne. I lied; the plate was for me. I was hooked.

One plate led to another. Antique shops, flea markets, and yard sales yielded more and more. Don and the girls bought me pieces for Christmas, Mother's Day, and my birthday. Several shipments came in from California, where Cathy our oldest daughter lived. We built shelves to display my treasures, cataloged them, read and learned more about them. I began to turn up my nose at less-than perfect pieces and to argue with vendors about prices. In short, I became a **Collector**.

But to paraphrase Robert Frost, "One could do worse than be a collector." There are worse weaknesses, and there are worse places to spend one's time than in a flea market.

I think dinnerware fanciers collect primarily because china is beautiful. We like the feel of the glaze, the beauty of the lines, and the charm of the decoration. We are also romantic enough to like the idea of continuity, a connection with our mothers and grandmothers. Women have always been nourishers, and the tables that we set, like the food that we set upon them, are to feed the soul as well as the body. To eat beans and weinies with old silver plate from porcelain plates and then dab away the mustard with soft old monogrammed linen is not foolish; it is civilized.

Collecting Harker or any other American dinnerware is also an expression of patriotism. Except for a few firms, the American pottery industry is extinct and is unlikely to be resurrected. The world in which every housewife could choose from the old-fashioned flowers of the Amy decal to

the deco-modern shape of Zephyr to express her personality in her dinnerware is over. Hall and Homer Laughlin keep turning out the same Autumn Leaves and Fiesta; and, lovely as Lennox china is, it is elegantly unchanging. The only other alternatives are plastics or imports.

Some people collect for curiosity, some for hope of profit, some for sentimental reasons, some for Heaven-knows-why. Only the second reason, I think, is foolish. Unless one is collecting gold or some other scarce commodity, collections usually have no intrinsic value. After all, if our civilization falls tomorrow, what use can I have for more than 500 pieces of ceramics?

Why do I collect Harker Pottery? Because it is fun. Finding a new cup or plate is like finding buried treasure. If the price of the treasure is not exorbitant, I add it to my trove. If the article is too expensive for my budget, I sigh and pass it by, taking home only the memory of a lovely object.

Sentiment, of course, has a great deal to do with collecting. I love my husband very much and Chester, West Virginia, the home of Harker Pottery from 1931 to its closing in 1972, was his hometown. His family and he were closely connected to the industry, so Harker is part of my children's heritage as well.

I also like pottery. It is both beautiful and useful, an almost irresistible combination. One of the oldest civilized arts, it is one of the most human arts, a part of everyone's daily life, the piece of clay that keeps our daily bread off the tablecloth and sets our habits above those of animals.

In addition, I like the stimulation of learning something new. I suppose that if I ever learned everything about Harker Pottery, I might grow bored, but as there is little chance of that event, I keep on collecting and learning.

As I began to learn more about the history of American potteries, I began to collect for another reason: Harker's is the archetypical American pottery, an example of and a major contributor to the industry. Not the finest pottery made in America, Harker's ware may be the best reflection of our history, of real, imperfect, pioneer families striving to earn a living and make a lasting contribution to this land. Every piece represents a moment in American history from the beginnings in 1840 of an immigrant entrepreneur through the struggles of a young, growing nation to the depths of the Depression and the burst of energy during and after World War II. Harker Pottery did not make expensive porcelain for the wealthy; they made everyday American ware for everyday Americans, but these dishes are mementos of another age.

Harker's story is also an American tragedy that we see repeated today. Long protected by tariffs and relatively cheap labor, the pottery industry in the United States succumbed to plastics, the demands of twentieth-century economics, and world politics. So each piece is also a little bit of America, a reminder of a day gone by that shall not return, when we felt ourselves preeminent and self-sufficient.

—Chapter One—
The Town That Clay Built

Where the Ohio River finally turns south, three states meet. Ohio lines the western bank, and Pennsylvania relinquishes its claim to the river-child born in Pittsburgh to West Virginia on the eastern bank. Wide and beautiful, *La Belle Riviere*, as French explorers called it, sweeps down a floodplain lined with hills that it has carved from the foothills of the Appalachian Mountains. Whenever the river channel curves, the hills often loom steeply over the outside banks that the current has cut into the stone and clay, and on the inside banks, floodplains of varying depths like shallow bowls are formed from the silt that the river has left behind. Beyond the western banks lie the fertile Ohio hills that eventually meet the Great Plains. The eastern bank outlines West Virginia, that beautiful, misunderstood, exploited state wrested from Virginia during the Civil War.

Covering the hills are remnants of hardwood forests. Where the river has cut away the hills, or where railroad beds and highways later were built, layers of coal and clay occasionally appear. Under the forests of hardwood trees lies rich soil to raise crops and grass for livestock. Under the soil lie deposits of clay, coal and natural gas: clay to be formed into ceramics of a thousand different uses; coal and gas to heat the kilns to fire the clay.

The river itself was both the greatest boon and greatest barrier to the pioneers. Untamed by dams or dredges, the Ohio was unpredictable. Riverboat captains told of being halted in times of drought by horses and wagons fording the stream. During plentiful rains, the river flooded the plains, sweeping away anything in its path. In the winter, it could freeze solid and no traffic moved. But "when she was good, she was very, very good," providing transportation for the produce of the land, the trees to build with, the coal to run the engines, and the clay to build a city.

It was the clay that brought James Bennett, an English potter, from Staffordshire to the bend in the river around 1839. Bennett had lived and worked in potteries in the East and the lower Ohio Valley, seeking the perfect place to establish a pottery for himself and his brothers who were to follow him to America. At the bend of the river were deposits of buff-burning clay that when fired became a light or golden yellow, perfect to cover with a clear glaze for yellow ware or with a rich brown to make Rockingham ware.

With financial backing from local businessmen and cheap (or free) clay from some of the farmers in the hills above the little town of East Liverpool, Ohio, Bennett built the first successful commercial pottery in what was to become the center of the ceramic industry in the United States.

Bennett flourished in East Liverpool long enough to bring his brothers over from England, until the river that brought him to the valley helped to drive him out. Discouraged by floods and ill health, Bennett moved his operations to Pittsburgh. In 1852 a flood swept away the last traces of his factory in East Liverpool, but he had made his valuable contribution to the area potteries and to our story. In 1926, when a bronze marker honoring Bennett was installed in the Carnegie Library in East Liverpool, Harker Pottery was among the sponsors.

According to some reports, the people of the little village of East Liverpool were not all wildly enthusiastic about Bennett's ambitions. Fire was a constant worry in a frontier town built of wood, and the kiln (pronounced "kill" by potters) caused some concern. As more potteries were built, fear must have increased. In 1846 an ordinance required all potteries inside the city limits to be surrounded by a forty-foot high brick wall. In addition, the factories were forbidden to keep straw inside buildings. An article written in 1939 stated that the laws were never repealed, but never enforced.

Ware was packed in straw for shipment in barrels, which the potteries often made themselves. As well as being a fire hazard, this practice resulted in a confusing system of sizing ware. If a bowl was sized "36S," thirty-six could be packed in a standard barrel.

One resident who sold clay to James Bennett was Benjamin Harker Sr. who with his wife Ann, two sons, and two daughters had come to the valley to farm. Harker, a slater or roofer, had sold everything in Dudley, Staffordshire, England, and traveled to America to buy land and live as a gentleman farmer. When he found large deposits of clay in the hills above the acreage that he bought for $3700 from Abel Coffin, he sold the clay to Bennett and also shipped it to Pittsburgh and other markets.

The clay in the hills had to be mined, exposed to the elements to crumble, ground into small pieces, sifted to remove stones, sticks, insects, and other contaminants, and mixed with water. The water leached out soluble impurities, and then the mixture was heated and drained to form malleable clay.

In one old story, young George Harker, Benjamin's older son, took a flatboat of clay down river to Cincinnati to sell. Unable to find a buyer, he was bemoaning his fail-ure when a runaway riverboat crashed into the docked flat-boat and sank it. The captain of the errant packet was eager to settle and paid George much more than the lost cargo and barge were worth.

Then in true American fashion, Benjamin Sr. decided that he could as easily make pottery as supply the clay. Harker built an ingenious system to haul the clay down from the hills, a six-foot beehive kiln, and a small work-shop near a log cabin that had formerly been used to make whiskey or beer. Harker's factory, built beside the river, was a mile north of the village in 1840 and just south of Babb Island, under what is today the Jennings Randolph Bridge which carries U.S. 30 westward across the Ohio River. Thus began what was to become the oldest continu-ally run pottery in the United States, one that contributed enormously to the growth of Ohio's pottery industry.

Benjamin Harker Sr. was not a potter, but an entrepreneur. He hired an experienced man, John Goodwin, to run the pottery and — more importantly to our story — to teach the craft to the Harker sons, George S. and Benjamin Jr. Although Goodwin left Harker's after an argument that resulted when an overheated kiln fused a load of ware into an unusable lump, he must have taught the Harker boys well, for the firm was to last more than 125 years. Harker's daughter Jane married David Boyce, the son of Richard Boyce, a neighboring farmer who had enter-tained the Harkers when they had first arrived. These were the flesh and blood that used the clay to build a small American dynasty.

Benjamin Sr. retired soon after founding his pottery. The actual date of his death is difficult to document from written records, and his tombstone is worn badly, but in

Plate 1. This plain brown mug from the archives of the Ohio Museum of Ceramics is attributed to Benjamin Harker,Jr. Approximately 5" high, it bears no backstamp or mark. $100.00.

Plate 2. One of the original Harker, Taylor hound-handled jugs. Note the detailed designs; the grape clusters around the top are make up of tiny individual beads of clay. Authority John Spargo called it "one of the best." Approximately 10" high and marked with the impressed raised circle of Harker, Taylor & Co. (ca. 1847-51.) From the archives of the Ohio Museum of Ceramics. $600.00.

1851 he signed a deed selling property to his son, so he was still alive then.

In this little, not-always-successful factory, many famous names in American pottery learned their trade. John Goodwin, who ran Harker's kilns and trained the Harker sons, went on to a distinguished career after he left Harker's. Isaac Knowles of Knowles, Taylor and Knowles (KT&K) worked as a carpenter in the village and helped build wooden machines to mix the clay. He also peddled pottery door to door for Harker and others before building his own kilns. A story in the East Liverpool newspaper in 1876 claims that only two of the eighteen other potteries in town were owned by men who had not worked at Harker's at some time or another.

Benjamin Harker's sons, Benjamin Jr. and George, were joined in 1846 by a partner, James Taylor.In addition to yel-low ware, toys, tiles, and door knobs, Harker, Taylor and Co. made Rockingham ware. This included hound-handled pitchers, one of which is displayed today in the Smithsonian Institution's Museum of American History. In 1850 Harker, Taylor and Co. won a silver medal for excel-lence from the Massachusetts Charitable Mechanic Association exhibition for its Rockingham ware. What is sig-nificant is that the award was presented in New England, the home of Bennington Pottery, famous for its Rockingham. ("Rockingham" refers to a type of pottery and glaze, not to a particular factory. "Bennington" refers to a city in New England where Rockingham was made. The two terms are not interchangeable.)

The pottery built in 1846 by the Harkers and Taylor was christened Etruria Pottery, according to some authori-ties in honor of — or more likely in imitation of — the

Wedgwood Pottery in Staffordshire, England. In the nineteenth and early twentieth centuries, American ceramics were considered innately inferior to European products, especially those of England. This attitude still lingers, but in the mid-1800's many American potteries went so far as to hide their origins. They used either no trademarks or marks that imitated English ones. So the name could have been an attempt to seem properly British.

On the other hand, Lucille Cox, who wrote a series of charming articles for the *East Liverpool Review* about Harker's, claims that the name was proposed by an unknown visitor at the celebration party for the new factory. This gentleman suggested that it be named for the province of Etruria, land of the Etruscans, who created lovely pottery in ancient times. Choose the story that seems most likely or most romantic to you.

Nevertheless, Harker and Taylor's Etruria Works was one of the few East Liverpool potteries to mark their yellow and Rockingham ware. George S. Harker Company, which later succeeded this partnership and others and eventually became Harker Pottery, in 1879 was one of the first to use the American flag as part of their backstamp, flaunting their patriotism. Much of the ware produced in East Liverpool before 1900 is difficult to attribute to a particular pottery, but the Etruria and Harker, Taylor and Co. impressed their trademark on the bottom of most of their ware.

James Bennett was not the only English potter to come to the United States in search of a better life. Many English artisans from Staffordshire and other British ceramic centers left England to escape unfair labor practices that kept the operatives virtual serfs. Many families in the Ohio Valley today trace their ancestry back to these immigrants, who brought a great tradition of craftsmanship to America. But the English influence on the style was changing slowly; a new, American style was emerging. In *American Potters*

and Pottery, Ramsay says, "West of the [Appalachian] mountains we find pottery which reflects the origin and training of its makers, but these are ... American, not European influences."

The Harker brothers took on several of these potters as both workers and, in a series of alliances that can be confusing, as partners. We do not know why the Harker brothers split up, formed new businesses, and then rejoined on several occasions, but East Liverpool and the Ohio Valley were booming. Cheap land, fuel, labor, transportation and raw materials, as well as the growing demand from the West and South, allowed the pottery industry and the area to flourish. Interested partners were always available, and the records of the Harker and Boyce families demonstrate that all had an eye for opportunity. Ramsay points out that during the late nineteenth century "nearly a hundred individuals, partnerships, and corporations succeeded each other in various combinations..., but it is interesting to note that the same names occur again and again."

Lois Lehner in her *Encyclopedia of U.S. Marks on Pottery, Porcelain, & Clay* wisely and humorously dismisses the problem of these changing partnerships:

> The pottery researchers do not agree at all on the dates of the early meanderings and partnerships of the Harkers, and I can't imagine Benjamin and his successors worrying very much about record-keeping as they fought the weather, primitive methods and bone weary tiredness, just trying to get that clay off the big hill and made into usable products.

I agree, but I will try to unravel the tangled relationships.

From 1840 to 1846 the firm had no recorded name and

Fig.1A

Fig.1B

Fig.1C

Fig. 1A. Drawn by Stradling from original impressed mark ca. 1840. Photocopied from *Lehner's Encyclopedia*. **Fig. 1B.** Drawn from original impressed mark. ca.1846-51. Photocopied from Ramsay. **Fig. 1C.** Drawn from original impressed mark. ca. 1846-51. Photocopied from Barber.

made yellow ware and Rockingham. From 1846 to 1851 (George and Benjamin Jr.) Harker, Taylor and Co. made prize-winning Rockingham and yellow ware. They impressed and embossed their marks. In 1850 this was one of the largest potteries in East Liverpool, according to Gates. From 1851 to 1854, George and Benjamin Jr., in partnership with Ezekiel Creighton and Mathew Thompson, formed Harker, Thompson and Company to make yellow ware and Rockingham. They won a "superior" medal for Rockingham and yellow ware from the American Institute of New York, and the ceramic business card that the partners created is on display in the Museum of Ceramics in East Liverpool today. Occasionally, the sign is listed as a mark in catalogs, but it is merely an ingenious advertising device, not a stamp or impressed mark. I have found no Harker, Thompson mark.

About this time, Benjamin Jr. left to form his own "Mansion Works" with partner William G. Smith. I cannot find the mark that they used, but Harker and Smith's business was short-lived, and Benjamin returned to the family firm within a few years. In 1854 or 1859, depending on the source, George bought out non-family partners and formed George S. Harker Company.

Plate 3. Not a mark, this "calling card" by Harker, Thompson and Company (ca. 1851-54) is on display at the Ohio Museum of Ceramics in East Liverpool.

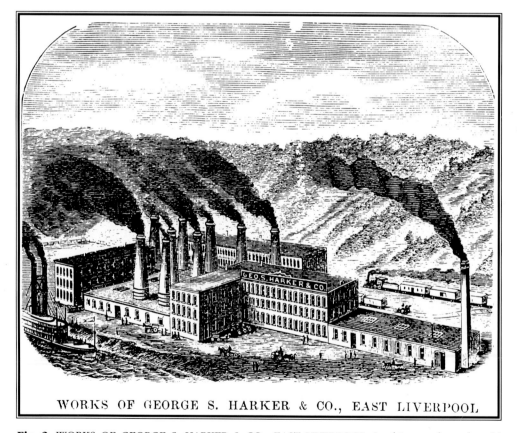

WORKS OF GEORGE S. HARKER & CO., EAST LIVERPOOL

Fig. 2. WORKS OF GEORGE S. HARKER & CO., EAST LIVERPOOL. In this woodcut, the old East Liverpool plant is seen at its height, complete with railroads and steamboats bringing in raw materials and carrying away the finished ware.

Benjamin Jr. joined the Union Army in 1863. Some references claim that he was drafted, but I like to think that he was a patriotic volunteer. After all, at 37 he must have been too old to be drafted, and he went so far as to name one of his sons Abraham Lincoln Harker. Also, in the Ohio Museum of Ceramics in East Liverpool is a small white bust of Lincoln attributed to Benjamin.

George S. Harker died a year later, leaving his widow Rachel with six children. David Boyce, sister Jane's husband, stepped in to run the pottery until George's sons were old enough. Benjamin Jr. returned to the family firm after the war, but in 1877, when nephew W. W. Harker took over the firm and was joined by his younger brother Hal, Uncle Benjamin and his sons sold all interest in the original firm to George's sons.

Benjamin and his sons formed Wedgewood Pottery. The extra letter *e* in the name may result from poor spelling or a deliberate attempt to differentiate between themselves and the English pottery. At any rate, Wedgewood was active for only four years before Benjamin Jr. sold out, reportedly because his sons were not interested in making

Fig. 4A   Fig. 4B

Fig. 4C

Fig. 4A-C. Monochrome stamps used on white ware ca. 1879-1890.

pottery. In addition to yellow and Rockingham, Wedgewood made cream-colored or c.c. ware. I have found no documented mark.

The brothers must have maintained friendly relations, for in 1881 the Etruria Pottery of George S. Harker and the Wedgewood Pottery of Benjamin Harker Jr. shared a picnic across the Ohio River at Rock Springs Grove in an area which was to become the town of Chester, West Virginia.

By this time, sister Jane Boyce's family had become an integral part of the George S. Harker Company, and the firm had begun to produce white ware. The change from yellow ware and Rockingham was prompted by public demand and, more immediately, a $5,000 prize put up by the town of East Liverpool for the first pottery to produce semi-porcelain. Semi-porcelain — whiter, harder, and less absorbent — had replaced the yellow ware and Rockingham in fashion. Harker didn't win the prize, but they did join the competition and the move to white ware. In 1890 when George S. Harker Company was incorporated into the Harker Pottery with W.W. Harker, George's oldest son, as its first president, Harker was producing both semi-porcelain and graniteware, heavy white ware popular with restaurants and hotels.

Fig. 3A

Fig. 3B

Fig. 3A. Impressed mark. ca. 1844-47. **Fig. 3B**. Impressed mark. ca. 1862.

—Chapter Two—
Nice Things

Most of the earliest ware Harker produced was utilitarian: mugs, bowls, plates, nappies (open vegetable bowls), milk pans, butter tubs, baking pans and chamber pots. All of these were yellow ware, for which the local clays were merely glazed or decorated with colored bands or with sponging, an uneven pattern of contrasting color applied with a sponge. Even though we cherish them today, the plates and baking pans were not meant to be luxuries. After all, a community a generation away from the frontier needed only the most basic pottery.

The Rockingham ware — buff clay glazed with dark brown — was frequently modeled into something closer to luxury. Rockingham glaze, produced by adding manganese, gave a unique pattern to each piece. No two were alike. Bright streaks of color were often produced by adding lead to the glaze.

Spittoons — including smaller, daintier "ladies' spittoons" — with paneled sides or shell designs replaced the practice of spitting out an open door or into the fireplace. Pitchers ("ewers" or "jugs" to potters), mugs, basins and purely decorative pieces appeared in various shades of brown with and without mottling, irregular color.

Most of the Rockingham designs were copied from Europe or New England. Hound-handled pitchers, Toby

Plate 5. A charming example of the popular Toby jugs by George S. Harker Co. ca. 1877. Ohio Museum of Ceramics. $250.00.

Plate 4. Rockingham spittoon with shell decoration by the George S. Harker Co. in the mid-nineteenth century. Ohio Museum of Ceramics. $150.00.

Plate 6. A 9" plain round dinner plate, $10.00; 13" plain oval platter, $15.00; and 11" fluted bowl (nappy), $20.00, are all stamped with the Embellished Bow and Arrow that marks most Harker ware from 1890 to 1930.

mugs, and spaniel dogs were favorites. The quality escalated quickly enough for Harker, Taylor and Company to win prizes competing against older, more established New England and New Jersey potteries. The low prices offered by the Ohio Valley potteries inevitably squeezed some older Eastern firms out of the market.

As the standard of living in America rose, the immigrants and their American-born children wanted more luxurious possessions. The longing for "nice things" is common to all women who want beauty as well as utility. Pretty curtains instead of wood shutters, rugs on a planked floor, and the shine of a treasured teapot or a decorative plate kept our grandmothers spiritually alive on the frontier.

In 1879 Harker began to make white ware: table, cooking, and sanitary ware made of white clays, flint, and kaolin imported from southern and border states rather than from the buff-burning clay of the region. By 1927 only one dinnerware pottery, D.E. McNichol, was using the clay that first brought James Bennett to the Ohio Valley. This change was made possible by the railroads that began to network the area. The Cleveland and Pittsburgh Railroad, constructed in 1852, brought in raw materials and distributed finished ware to western, southern, and even eastern markets previously reserved for New England and New Jersey potteries. A spur of the railroad, built privately by a cartel of East Liverpool potters, extended in 1856 to Harker's Pottery on the river for easy access to riverboats.

The first semi-porcelain that George S. Harker Company produced was rather plain, but its production was an occasion for celebration. According to legend, the

Fig. 5A

Fig. 5B

The arrow, that with a bow was to become Harker's established mark, appears here for probably the first time. **Fig. 5A**. Monochrome used on granite ware ca. 1890-1904. **Fig. 5B**. Monochrome used on semivitreous ware ca. 1890-1930.

whole Harker work force was ferried across the river on the *John Darling* to Rock Springs Grove, the predecessor of the famous Rock Springs Park, for a beer-barrel picnic, accompanied by the East Liverpool Brass Band. I don't know if the legend is true, but if not, it should be.

Utilitarian, everyday ware was Harker's forte, and some of the oldest pieces I own are bowls. I particularly treasure a wide, shallow, plain white bowl in the Republic shape stamped with the George S. Harker crossed flags mark. Although I know that it is unlikely, I like to imagine that it is part of the first white ware produced in 1879 that inspired the pottery owners and workers to celebrate at Rock Springs.

Later, embossed patterns and colorful decals were added to the plain white semi-porcelain and granite ware. Many people refer to this hard, glossy white ware as "stoneware," but very little real stoneware -- a term usually reserved for the blue-gray ware of Great Britain -- was made in East Liverpool.

These early shapes were given names for marketing purposes: Bedford was a line of severely rectangular tableware with ornate handles. Dixie was softly scalloped at the edges, and the hollow ware was fluted to look like a collection of columns. Cable was decorated in a popular rope-like relief.

Romantic names fill the old Harker catalogs: Waverly, Lorain, Fairfax, French, Paris, and Rocaille, which is a French word for ornate scrolls and was used again more than fifty years later. Manila was probably named for the Spanish-American War, Menlo for Thomas Edison, Western for Teddy Roosevelt's fascination with the West, and Windsor about the time that the British Royal family Anglicized their names. Republic has a distinctive finial of a cross inside a circle. But as if to remind the collector that names were irrelevant to the potter, one old catalog lists "Semi-porcelain" as a shape.

"Sanitary ware" included wash basins, large water pitchers (called ewers), toothbrush holders (brush vases), smaller hot water pitchers (mouth pitchers), shaving mugs, slop jars, bedpans, and feeders for infants and invalids. Toilet sets made up of basin, ewer, brush vases, pitchers, shaving mugs, and slop jars (chambers, cabinets or cuspidores as they were coyly called) were embellished with embossed curlicues and scalloped edges, decorated with floral decals, and finished off with gold lines or with spattered gold edgings.

Although a salesman's hand-tinted photograph lists designs on ewers and basins by numbers only, more alluring titles were given to other lines of sanitary ware. Ornate Manila featured sprays of acanthus leaves or perhaps feathers. Etruria was a classic amphora-shaped toilet set. Iolanthe, a toilet ware line embellished with medallions, had its own backstamp, and the Argonaut toilet set introduced the ribbed collar to Harker products.

Plate 7. White ware Republic shape vegetable bowl bears the Crossed Flags mark of George S. Harker Company. $20.00.

Plate 8. The spoon rest, $25.00, is in the Republic shape and bears the George S. Harker Crossed Flags. The leaf-shaped plate, $49.00, was probably used for candies or other decorative uses and carries the George S. Harker Ironstone China stamp. Ohio Museum of Ceramics.

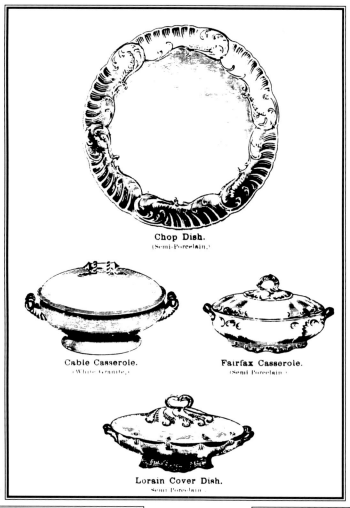

Chop Dish.
(Semi-Porcelain.)

Cable Casserole.
(White Granite.)

Fairfax Casserole.
(Semi Porcelain.)

Lorain Cover Dish.
(Semi-Porcelain.)

Fig. 6A

EAST LIVERPOOL, O.   21

All Prices are by the Dozen except where stated per Gross.

BEDFORD.
New Square-Shape.

SUGARS.

24s..$5 75

TEA POTS.

24s..$7 00

Fig. 6B

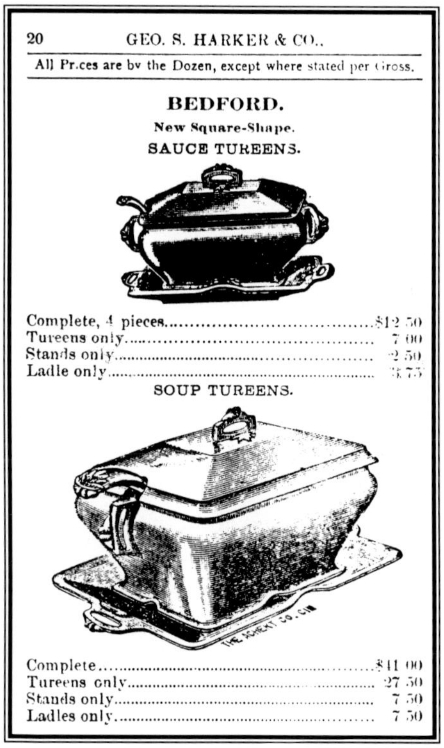

20   GEO. S. HARKER & CO.,

All Prices are by the Dozen, except where stated per Gross.

BEDFORD.
New Square-Shape.
SAUCE TUREENS.

Complete, 4 pieces...............................$12 50
Tureens only.. 7 00
Stands only.. 2 50
Ladle only... 3 75

SOUP TUREENS.

Complete...$41 00
Tureens only.. 27 50
Stands only.. 7 50
Ladles only.. 7 50

Fig. 6C

Fig. 6A-C. The Bedford, Cable, Fairfax, Lorain shapes and the plate shape identified only as Semi-Porcelain. From Harker sales catalogs ca. 1890-1900. Ohio Museum of Ceramics.

Fig. 7A

Fig. 7B

Fig. 7C

Fig. 7A-C. The Etruria, Iolanthe, and Argonaut toilet sets. From Harker catalogs ca. 1890-1900. Ohio Museum

Fig.8A

Fig. 8B

Fig. 8C

Fig. 8A-C. Manila, Menlo, and Miami Toilet sets. From Harker catalogs ca. 1890-1900. Ohio Museum of Ceramics.

HOTEL

Fig. 9A   **Fig. 9B**

Fig. 9A. Monochrome stamp on sanitary granite ware ca. 1879-90. **Fig. 9B**. Monochrome stamp on granite ware ca. 1890-1920.

Plate 9

The ewer and matching dresser tray with Elk decal and a brown blush graced a bedroom almost a hundred years ago. The basin is of another pattern that I call Green Rocaille. The ewer and basin were called the Western shape, a line restricted to these sets. Of course, they form a "marriage," a set that is made up of two different patterns, and a bad marriage at that. The dresser tray is Dixie shape.

Both the lid of the chamber pot with its peach roses and lilacs and the base with its painted daisies are the same shape -- Manila -- but this is probably also a marriage. The brush vase, unadorned except for gold lines, is Manila, but the shaving mug, with pastel roses, is from the Cable line; a small cross inside a circle decorates the handle.

Plate 10

Plate 9. Elk ewer, $65.00, and dresser tray, $20.00; Green Rocaille basin, $65.00. **Plate 10**. Manila brush vase, $10.00, and chamber pot, $40.00; Pasel Roses shaving mug, $30.00.

Transfer printing was one technique used to decorate early white ware. The design was printed on the body in monochrome and then color was added by hand. This Moss Rose decoration was almost generic in the era; many potteries used it.

More colored and metallic embellishments soon were added to Harker's ware. One popular theme was the Cabbage Rose: lush red, pink, and gold roses. Another favorite device was a technique of spraying on contrasting color in "blushes" in a variety of tinted glazes.

The plate below with the yellow roses is "signed"; that is, the decal was signed by its creator. Later in this chapter is another signed piece, a platter with a Pheasant decal. Knowing the designer's name is interesting, but both patterns are still merely decals, used on thousands of items, not individually crafted works. Many collectors confuse these decals with signed hand-painting.

Most of the plates below were probably used as decorations. The one at top right is a souvenir. The tumbler could be part of a lemonade set. The vase, based on the Regal shape, was made later than most of the other pieces; it carries the 1840 Bow and Arrow Mark rather than the Embellished Bow and Arrow. The bowl on the lower right is an advertising premium with a commercial message on the back.

Plate 11. Sugar bowl in unidentified shape with Moss Rose transfer design is stamped with the Stone China/HP bow and arrow. Ohio Museum of Ceramics. $65.00.

Plate 12. Top row: Cabbage Rose dinner plate, $10.00; Green Blush tumbler, $10.00; Green Blush tray on Dixie shape, $20.00; Souvenir plate, $20.00. Bottom row: Cabbage Rose on scalloped dinner plate, $10.00; Cabbage Rose signed-decal plate, $20.00; Parrot vase on Regal shape, $25.00; Blue Grapes pie baker, $15.00; Advertising bowl with Strawberries decal, $15.00.

Some early twentieth-century Harker pieces that we found in the Ohio Museum of Ceramics while researching this book were breathtaking or unbelievable. This dresser tray in glowing turquoise with luscious Cabbage Roses took my breath away, and I couldn't believe that Harker made the Strawberries and Gold demitasse set.

Incorporated as Harker Pottery in 1898, the family-owned business seemed to be thriving but was not without its problems. Cheap raw materials and fuel, a skilled labor force, a growing technology, and strong protective tariffs gave East Liverpool businesses a decided advantage over other American potteries, allowing them to undersell the New Jersey and New England firms. However, "Crockery City" was a one-industry town with 90 percent of its citizens employed in the potteries or related industries, leaving it vulnerable to financial and political reversals.

Plate 14. Cabbage Roses on turquoise dresser tray. Ohio Museum of Ceramics. $100.00.

Plate 13. Strawberries and Gold Demitasse set. Ohio Museum of Ceramics. $125.00.

Plate 15. The Frogs and Scarecrow plate, $30.00, and Playmates cylindrical dish, $40.00, are stamped with the Embellished Bow and Arrow, but the Dog and Bunny set, $35.00, dates from later and has the 1840 Bow.

Like Americans today, early consumers wanted to give their children the best. Those fat, lace-bedecked babies staring out of old tintypes may not have been born with silver spoons in their mouths, but many were fed from special dishes. Often the decals on the dishes are badly faded and scratched by Mother's urging Baby to eat the last morsel.

Fig. 10A   Fig. 10B   Fig. 10C

Harker's classic bow and arrow mark evolves. **Fig. 10A**. Monochrome mark used on granite ware and semi-porcelain ca. 1890-1900. **Fig. 10B**. Monochrome mark used on granite ware and semi-porcelain ca. 1890-1910. **Fig. 10C**. This Embellished Bow and Arrow mark (ca. 1890-1930) is the most frequently used mark on older Harker semi-porcelain.

The protective tariffs were often at the mercy of political battles. Recessions have always hurt the pottery industry badly, and the Civil War ruined many firms when they lost their Southern markets and the port of New Orleans, through which they exported. In addition, the expansion of technology that brought in mass-production methods attracted cheaper unskilled labor. To protect themselves, the potters had to organize, bringing labor strife to the valley.

Frankly, workers were badly treated, sometimes paid in ware or with chits, I.O.U.s redeemable at local businesses. Labor wanted and needed low tariffs and cheap consumer goods to live on, but owners wanted high tariffs to protect the potteries and therefore the workers' livelihoods. This situation produced a sad political schism. By 1912 the National Brotherhood of Operative Potters had unionized all American potteries after a long era of strikes and lock-outs.

Workers and owners alike wanted to enjoy the fruits of their labor or investments. Sometimes, the designs that they chose to decorate the ware reflected the American bounty: fruits, fish, and game of all kinds like these below.

However, work in the potteries in the mid-1800's was "dirty, tedious, laborious, and often grueling," says Gates.

Silicosis or "potter's consumption" was common. Women and children worked the same hours as men for less money; one girl-child set fire to her employer's plant because she hated the work. The potteries were originally unheated, so the work was seasonal, not to protect the workers from chilblains, but to protect the clay from freezing. Harker was one of first to solve the problem well enough to work through the winter, although I can find no details about their solution.

By 1931 one big problem was solved: the seasonal battle with the Ohio River. Before the river was tamed by a system of dams and locks, it fluctuated between flood and drought. In 1854 the water was so low that nothing could be shipped; in other years the potteries were flooded. In the Ohio Historical Society's Museum of Ceramics in East Liverpool is an undecorated formerly covered dish with its lid missing. The dish was left behind by raging waters that swept through Harker's in 1884. Surveying the damage when the water receded, W.W. Harker found the unfired piece. He had it inscribed: "One of 6 covered dishes/Only batch ware left in green house after flood of Feb. 7, 1884," and had it fired as a grim souvenir. In 1931 Harker solved this problem by moving to higher, drier ground across the river.

Plate 16. The Fruits of their Labor. Top row: Fruits plate, $20.00; Signed Pheasants decal platter, $30.00; Apples and Nuts plate, $10.00. Bottom row: Cherry Blossom dinner plate, $10.00; Peaches fruit dish, $5.00; Cherry Blossom tray, $15.00.

—Chapter Three—
Floods, Fire, Famine

Its geography, which helped East Liverpool become the source of much twentieth-century American dinnerware, was the city's fortune and its burden. The hills, which supplied the first clay for the kilns and the coal and natural gas to keep them burning, limited the town's expansion. The river, which carried the clay, coal, and finished ceramics, rose regularly to flood the factories.

Harker Pottery, built on the river's edge with the hills rising directly behind it, was hampered by its originally favorable location. In 1844, 1852, and 1913 the river had flooded disastrously. Again and again the Ohio River put out the fires in the kilns. Sometimes the fires did not go out; one old photo in the Museum of Ceramics shows Specialty Glass Company in flames but cut off from the fire engines by floodwaters.

In addition, as Harker's business grew, the plant had no room to expand. The firm had already bought the National China Plant and the adjacent six-kiln plant of Homer Laughlin, but by the end of the second decade of the twentieth century, Harker's owners knew that they must expand again. Technology and their own success were strangling them in their old quarters.

Across the Ohio River lay the little town of Chester, West Virginia. Much of Chester sits high on a bluff, and the village was relatively undeveloped with room for expansion. Taylor, Lee and Smith (later Taylor, Smith & Taylor or TS&T) and the Edwin M. Knowles Pottery had already left East Liverpool. Indeed, Knowles had recently abandoned one factory in Chester to move again several miles south to Newell, West Virginia. In 1931 Harker quit "Crockery City," the town that it had helped to build, and moved into the old Knowles pottery.

Chester had been founded on speculation of the expansion of the thriving potteries across the river. The little town's Rock Springs Park, popular excursion destination and resort in the late nineteenth and early twentieth centuries, had been the scene of many of Harker's holiday picnics. However, until 1897 the only way across the wide Ohio was by ferry.

Land speculators, including the Harker and Boyce families, wanted a bridge built from East Liverpool to Chester. When the city fathers of East Liverpool refused to grant access to College Avenue for the bridge, Rachel Harker, widow of George S. Harker, stepped in and sold the builders some of her property. The roadway exiting the bridge on the Ohio side made an abrupt turn because of

this situation; nevertheless, the first of several bridges to connect Chester and East Liverpool was finished on New Year's Day 1897.

Interestingly, after the move to Chester, Harker kept its East Liverpool mailing address and used "East Liverpool, Ohio" on many of its marks. The prestige of being part of East Liverpool's history was worth too much to relinquish.

But they had what they wanted: safety from flood waters and room to expand. Even the 1936 flood, the greatest and most disastrous of the twentieth century, didn't touch Harker's. And the new Harker plant was more modern than the one that was founded by Benjamin Harker and his sons in 1840, even after almost a century of rebuilding and remodeling.

In an attempt to broaden their markets, in 1930 Harker created Columbia China Company with its own trademark, the Statue of Liberty, both in color and monochrome. Gates and Ormerod give the date 1910 for the monochrome stamp, and for some reason that I cannot explain, the date on the stamp claims that Columbia was founded in 1873. All these discrepancies aside, Columbia was most active during the Depression era.

Plate 17. On display at the Ohio Museum of Ceramics is this plain white plate marked "Last ware made Harker No. 2 - 1931." NFS.

Fig. 11A   **Fig. 11B**   **Fig. 11C**

Columbia Marks. **Fig. 11A**. Monochrome stamp ca. 1930-35. **Fig. 11B**. Color decal mark ca. 1930-35. **Fig. 11C**. Overstamp of color Columbia over Harker 1840 Bow and Arrow.

The ware sold by Columbia was the same as that sold under the Harker marks, and occasionally the Columbia stamp was added over top of the Harker stamp. Legend has it that many customers preferred Columbia's ware to that marked Harker. Part of the reason for this may be due to the retail stores where the pottery was sold. Using a variety of backstamps and creating a separate sales organization permitted Harker to sell "exclusive" lines to more than one retailer in an area. So, if a housewife bought her Columbia at a popular store and her Harkerware at a less-prestigious one, she may have become convinced that there was a difference in the dishes.

This may sound a little deceitful, but one must remember, first of all, that such practices are common even today and, most of all, that the United States at the time was in the midst of the Great Depression.

The Harker and Boyce families tried to take care of their workers during these hard years. Work was divided up according to occupations and orders, so that everyone had some time on the payroll. As the Depression deepened, Harker ran only a couple of days a week and paid workers in scrip good "when cash is available." The Ohio Pottery Museum has several of these drafts dated in 1933 and signed by H.R. (Hal) Harker and C. R. Boyce. Harker Pottery boasted that they never missed a pay, but Hal Harker, a grandson of Benjamin Harker Sr. and active in the pottery until he was 80 and blind, told friends that he often lay awake at night worrying about meeting the payroll, and many firms had to return to the old practice of paying workers in pottery or in chits for local stores that accepted ware in exchange.

A student of marketing could learn much by following Harker's advertising and sales practices. At the beginning of the century, Harker ware was still sold door-to-door, but the firm soon began using mail-order, advertising punch cards, and other promotions. The large department stores that replaced small general stores stocked Harker in their housewares departments.

In the '50s, when plastics began to squeeze the ceramics industry, Harker's ads bragged that their products were "odorless and sanitary as only true ceramic dinnerware can be," sniping at plastic's property of retaining odors, stains, and — so they suggest — germs.

The sale of premiums to businesses trying to boost their products by giving away "free china" helped, of course. Most motion picture theaters in the country gave away china on "Dish Night," and a family could accumulate a whole set if they attended regularly.

Plate 18. Calico Ribbon G.C. bowl, $20.00 and flat cake plate, $15.00; Basket of Flowers trivet, $10.00; Jewel Weed custards, $2.00 and casserole, $7.00 (flawed).

Columbia survived until 1955. Many charming older patterns decorate the ware, including, according to some authorities, Autumn Leaf for Jewel Tea Company. The cake plate and matching mixing bowl in Plate 18 are in Calico Ribbon (called Plaid in the decorating department), which was also made in brown, yellow and green. The stamps on the bottoms of the set do not match; the platter has a Columbia stamp, but the bowl is marked SunGlow

Bakerite. The trivet/ashtray with the Basket of Flowers is an unusual shape for Harker, who generally used an octagon for this purpose. The cylindrical casserole and custards pictured have a pattern that I called Morning Glory until I learned that Harker used that name for a design on a Royal Gadroon cake set in the '40s. Now I call it Jewel Weed, although the resemblance is dubious.

American Engobe
MADE BY HARKER
U. S. A.

Fig. 12A

Early American
By Harker
Est. 1840

Fig. 12B

Royal Dresden
by Harker
Est. 1840

Fig. 12C

Used for semi-porcelain dinnerware designs were these three marks in script. **Fig. 12A**. Monochrome ca. 1955-65. **Fig. 12B**. Monochrome ca. 1930-40. **Fig. 12C**. Monochrome ca. 1930-40.

Plate 19. Cathy vegetable bowl, $10.00; Orange Blossoms Gem cream and sugar set, $15.00; Carla plain oval platter, $10.00; Asters miniature Regal/Gargoyle jug, $20.00; Lisa standard jug, $25.00.

The pieces in this chapter were made between 1930 and the end of World War II as nearly as I can document. The pitchers or jugs in Plate 19 are called either Regal or Gargoyle. The large one has Lisa pattern; the smaller one I call Asters. The cream and sugar set with its Orange Blossoms decal is Gem shape. Because I have not discovered the names for some designs, I named them for my loved ones. Cathy is the orange and white poppies on the vegetable bowl, and Carla the yellow and gray pattern on the platter for my two older daughters.

The pitcher, Plate 20, in what I call Crayon Apples, was part of a waffle set, consisting of a platter, a large batter pitcher, and a smaller syrup jug. The platter for the waffles was usually in the Virginia shape, the round-cornered square, with handles or "lugs" like the big Lovelace plate in the center below. Both pitchers had lids in a teardrop shape. Complete sets are almost impossible to find, and the pitchers are frequently badly stained, but it is possible to reassemble one of these once-popular gift sets. Blanche is the multicolored design on the embossed-edge plate, and Lillian is the pattern on the green-lined plate: my mother-in-law and mother. Holly and Berries is a classic Christmas pattern. The abstract floral pattern on the Melrose plate I call Papyrus.

Plate 20. Blanche dinner plate, $5.00; Crayon Apples batter jug, $15.00; Lovelace Virginia utility platter, $20.00; Holly and Berries lunch plate, $8.00; Lillian dinner plate, $5.00; Papyrus Melrose dinner plate, $8.00.

The shallow floral soup bowl on the left in Plate 21 I call Corinne for my youngest daughter. The Windmill decal was used by several other potteries. The little Gem creamer and the Melrose souvenir plate both carry the same decoration that I call Blue Basket. The Basket of Flowers vegetable bowl at left front is more ornately decorated than usual for Harker.

The use of a decal or decalcomania on ware obviously broadened the possible decorations. All these lovely designs were printed on paper!

Of course, it was specially treated paper and the designs were transferred from the paper to the ware and then fired. Face down, the tissue-backed motif was affixed to the ware with varnish. After the fixative dried, the decal was soaked with water and scrubbed with bristle brushes to remove the paper, leaving only the colored design behind. After it was fired in the decorating kilns, the pattern was relatively permanent. Decals could be applied over the final glaze or under. A decal under the glaze is safer from damage, but less brilliant in color. Most of the decals on Harker were applied over the glaze.

Several kinds of decals were and are manufactured, but the best decals, I have been told, were from Germany, and American manufacturers soon turned to producing only water-transferable decals for other uses. Most designs were sold from catalogs from which any firm could choose, so this accounts for the duplication of patterns by several potteries. Of course, exclusive designs could be and were made and sold.

Printed on large sheets, the decals could be cut apart and applied in various patterns. They were made into strips to fit around the edge of a bowl or in blocks to fill the center of a plate. Sometimes a large part of the decal was cut away to fit an odd shape, or small sections were cut and placed inside a cup or bowl like a tiny beauty mark. Valma Baxter, who supervised the decorating department at Harker's for many years, kept log books of designs as did her counterparts in other factories. In these books, samples of the cut-up decals were pasted along with detailed directions for their use. The one remaining log book Valma kept solved several mysteries for me, and I wish that the others had not been destroyed.

Plate 21. Corinne soup dish, $6.00; Basket of Flowers vegetable dish, $15.00; Windmill lunch plate, $8.00; Blue Basket Gem creamer, $5.00; Blue Basket souvenir plate, $5.00.

Thriftily, the odds and ends of decal sheets were used up on "thirds," ware that could not pass inspection and therefore was usually not stamped. If work was slow in the decorating shed, Burt Harker, great-grandson of the founder, would give the decorators orders to use up the bits and pieces on thirds. Using their imagination and often combining patterns, the decorators trimmed flawed ware to be sold by the truckload to various vendors.

The decorating department applied the decals and the marks as well as adding embellishments like lining or other brush-applied additions. The stamps were specified in the log book too. The rubber impressions for the stamps were ordered from a specialty supplier, and then trimmed and attached to foam rubber and wood bases.

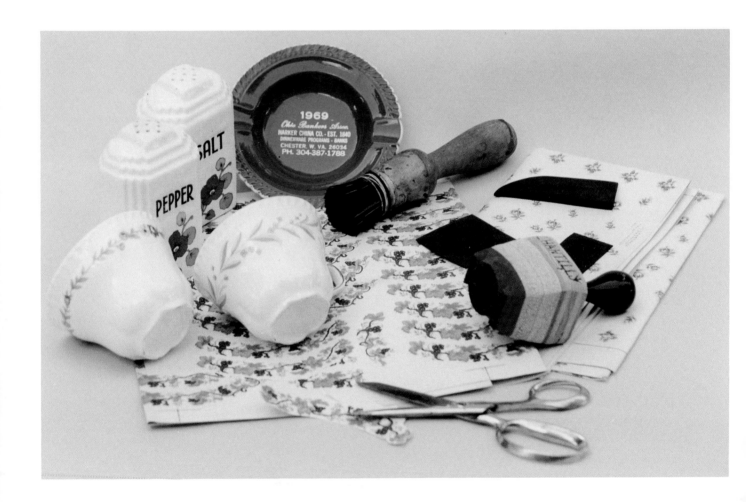

Plate 22. The tools of the trade. Sheets of Vintage on the left and Rosebud on the right are covered with various decorating tools. The brush was used to remove the wet paper backing and the rubber spatulas to smooth wrinkles from lift-off decals. An ashtray, $3.00, waits to be stamped with the Harker trademark, and a Bouquet (left) and a Ragwort cup (right), $5.00, pass inspection. The shakers, $10.00, are Nasturtium, a design that was never stamped.

Plate 23. Blue and Gold Band fruit dish, $5.00; Winter Asters Semi-Porcelain dinner plate, $15.00; Gold Diamonds cream and sugar set, $25.00; Regency Lovers dinner plate, $15.00; Strawberries dinner plate, $10.00; Wedding Bands saucer, $2.00.

Not all Harker ware of the early and middle twentieth century was brightly colored. The Winter Asters plate on the Semi-Porcelain shape, Plate 23, is demure and slightly old-fashioned. Regency Lovers in shades of plum is decorous. Even the gold-embellished plate with the Strawberries decal is not garish. The little fruit dish that I call Blue Band carries a jobber's stamp as well as Harker's. The cream and sugar set was auctioned off by a farm grange that served many dinners on Gold Diamonds, and the saucer is in a severely classic pattern that I call Wedding Bands.

One gambit to improve their fortunes during the Depression that Harker's owners did not attempt was merging or selling out. When the short-lived (1929-1932) American Chinaware was formed, Harker declined to join. The conglomerate's failure was a blow to the industry, according to Gates, but in an interview in 1983 Robert Boyce called the group "a bunch of sick chickens." I wonder if this was hindsight or the fact that Harker's had learned a lesson from their early history of short-lived partnerships.

—Chapter Four—
Gifts and Giveaways

From the turn of the century to the Depression years, imprinted pottery was a favorite advertising device, and Harker created much of it. The dishes, cups, and other pieces were welcomed in the recipients' homes and used frequently, but unfortunately for collectors, many were damaged or destroyed through use. Designs range from the beautiful to the charmingly naive and all are perfect collectors' items.

My favorite item in my collection is a calendar plate from 1907, the year both my parents were born. I had seen the quaint Santa and holly decals in Jo Cunningham's *Encyclopedia of American Dinnerware* and had loved them. Probably part of a very limited run, the calendar plate was for a Sunday School class: "Class 23, 9:30 every Sunday morning." It is also the only Harker plate I have

ever found with holes for attaching a hanger. This leads me to believe that it was made by or for someone in the pottery.

The imprinted verse reads:
> We are writing day by day,
>   Records which the Master reads;
> Why not illustrate each page
>   With a group of Golden Deeds?

Another inspirational piece is on a plate that I found in Massachusetts at a time when I needed just such a message:

I believe in today. It is all that I possess. The past is of value only as it can make the life of today fuller and freer. There is no assurance of tomorrow. I must make good today. -- Charles Steele[?]

Plate 24. Both the Novelty Poppies, $30.00, and the Holly and Berries Calendar Plates, $75.00, plates bear the Embellished Bow and Arrow.

Plate 25. In a variety of shapes, these Novelty Plates all bear the Embellished Bow and Arrow. "Aspirations," $20.00; Betsy Ross, $15.00; Pastoral, $30.00; Dog, $15.00; Indian, $25.00.

These patterns and messages may seem corny to today's reader, but they were made for the gift trade of another, more sentimental generation. Man's best friend and a pastoral scene of cattle grace two older shapes. Betsy Ross sews her first flag. An Indian on horseback wonders "What next?" as he watches a biplane pass over. A barefoot boy in a cornfield dreams of the White House. These were not meant to be used, but to inspire and to affirm one's beliefs.

This portrait plate, Plate 26, is the only one by Harker that I have ever seen. According to one apocryphal story, the women who posed for these popular decorations were no ladies except perhaps as in "ladies of the evening." Supposedly, since no respectable lady would pose — especially with so much flesh exposed — the artists hired women whose reputations would not suffer. I doubt the story; these are probably idealized portraits of imaginary women, but it does lend some spice to my collection.

Plate 26. Gypsy Portrait plate carries the Embellished Bow and Arrow, $28.00.

Plate 27. Souvenirs. Except for the octagonal trivet, which has a Columbia stamp, all of these souvenirs bear the older Embellished Bow and Arrow mark and date from the first decades of this century. $2.00-18.00.

I never buy a souvenir unless I am willing to hang it in my living room, so my favorite travel keepsakes are plates that Harker made for the tourist trade of long ago. I especially treasure ones that were made for places that my husband and I have enjoyed, but I have bought many from unknown towns because I liked the design. I have even gone so far as to buy the souvenir first and visit the town later.

Because we like the outdoors and camping, I love designs with wildlife scenes, and Harker must have made literally millions of them. These are mostly from New England, the East Coast, and the Midwest, but I am sure I will find many more when we travel in the South and West. The Indian maiden on her unusual ribbed-rim plate and the Indian chief, for instance, grace souvenirs from a half dozen or more American towns.

Plate 28. Wildlife Souvenirs. All carry the Embellished Bow and Arrow mark. $3.00-18.00.

Plate 29. Two hand-painted Virginia Gadroon souvenirs and two variations of the Godey decal on Virginia and Round Gadroon. $2.00-10.00.

Harker also sold a great many undecorated glazed plates to jobbers — artisans who decorated them for sale under their own marks. Many of these bear no backstamp, but later some of the Virginia Gadroon, a squared-off shape with a rope-like edge, were stamped with the Square Cartouche or a later variation of the bow and arrow. Sadly, these hand-paintings applied over the glaze are very delicate and are scratched easily.

Fig. 13A   Fig. 13B   Fig. 13C

Fig. 13A-C. These three variations of the Square Cartouche (ca. 1955-60) were used on almost every kind of ware.

The attractive Virginia and Round Gadroon shapes also were used by Harker to carry decals of state and tourist areas. Many souvenir plates or cup-and-saucer sets were sold unstamped to gift shops. Someday, I hope to collect all fifty states, backstamps or no backstamps.

Almost any business could and did give away advertising pottery as gifts or as premiums for a purchase. The potteries themselves promoted schemes to sell more dinnerware. Harker used coupons and punch card devices and gave away bonuses to boost sales. To promote the HotOven line, they gave a free "handled and lipped bowl" with purchases.

Advertising giveaways provide a great variety of styles and decorations for the collector. Again, I usually buy because I like the design or because I have visited the city, but some items are also good examples of a bygone fad or fashion. The ashtray for the bank in Plate 34 is an example of the popularity of pink and gray in the late '50s.

Plate 30 and 31. Both plates are backstamped and are from the Ohio Museum of Ceramics.

Plate 30. Church plate, $4.00.

Harker also made blanks for plates with drawings of churches that were popular as congregational fund-raisers, but I was surprised to find this commemorative plate marking the visit of Queen Elizabeth II and Prince Philip to the United States in 1957. On the back is printed: "Commemorating The Royal Visit of H.M. Queen Elizabeth II And H.R.H. Prince Philip To These United States."

Plate 31. Queen Elizabeth II Commemorative Plate, $25.00.

Plate 32. Calendar plates. 1915 Panama Canal plate, $22.00; 1913 Advertising plate, $25.00; 1960 Heritance plate, $5.00; 1929 Advertising trivet, $30.00; 1913 Advertising plate, $25.00.

Calendar plates, which date in America from about 1907, continued to be popular into the second half of the twentieth century. The most charming calendar plates are the old ones. The 1929 tea trivet/calendar is also an advertising device. The inscription is badly faded, but it seems to be made for a hardware store somewhere in Ohio. Two —

the horses and the cottage — are from a firm in Wheeling, West Virginia, my home town, and the 1915 commemorates the opening of the Panama Canal. I have found one Harker calendar plate on the Heritance shape from as late as 1960 for my eldest daughter, but none yet for her younger sisters.

Plate 33. Fontainebleau Hotel, $2.00-10.00.

Plate 34. Ashtrays. Left to right: Cap and Whip Club and Americana Inc. on plain round ashtrays. Bank on cylindrical shape. Game Birds; Silver Dollar; Harker Pottery on Round Gadroon. Only the Cardinal ashtray on the brass stand and the Game Birds are not advertisements. $2.00-10.00.

In an age before the surgeon general's report on smoking, ashtrays were often favorite gifts and souvenirs. Harker advertised themselves with an ashtray. I even saw, but did

not buy, an ashtray made for a Senior Girl Scout event. I trust the girls used the ashtrays for bobby pins.

Plate 36. Advertising plates. A deer is "Surprised;" Old Glory waves above an advertisement; a Fox and his prey share "A Critical Moment;" a Bunny leaves prints in the snow; a herd of sheep are "Thoroughbreds." All carry the Embellished Bow and Arrow. $3.00-30.00.

Paul Pinney, a long-time supervisor for Harker, told me that the pottery made 2,000 ashtrays for the opening of the Fontainebleau Hotel in Miami, Florida. All 2,000 mysteriously disappeared before a week was out, and the hotel had to order replacements. In spite of the fact that there must be many around somewhere, I had to wait years to find one.

Traditional themes like wildlife, patriotism, and rural scenes were popular designs for wall decorations. Even the smallest of businesses in the smallest of towns could keep their messages at their customers' eye level. Those on the far left and right as well as the second from the right in Plate 34 are in sepia tones.

Plate 36. The iridescent border is actually pale green, impossible to reproduce. Both Summer (left), and Autumn (right), $10.00 each, carry the Embellished Bow and Arrow.

Plate 37. This series of small dishes is marked on the back: "East Liverpool Merchants Welcome You. Fares Refunded Every Wednesday and Friday Throughout the Year." All bear the Embellished Bow and Arrow. Ohio Museum of Ceramics. $20.00 each.

Plates were the most common advertising devices, but not always. The pitcher with Oriental decorations probably was a premium given for a purchase or for opening an account. Harker made millions of refrigerator jars and jugs for Kelvinator in a variety of sizes, usually with the raised chevron of the G.C. line, but other potteries also made these for Kelvinator. (I wish I could explain a water jug on the Kelvinator shape with the Colonial Lady decal — a Harker exclusive, or so I thought! — with a Sebring stamp. Such are the mysteries of collecting china.) The Oriental Poppy vase is the only piece that I have been able to find that Harker probably made for the florist trade. I have been assured that there are more, but I have not found them.

Plate 38. The Oriental Poppy vase, $15.00, and the Oriental jug, $20.00, carry the 1840 Arrow, but the flawed Kelvinator refrigerator jar, $8.00, bears the HotOven color mark.

The advertising plaque in Plate 39 is based on Harker's traditional trivet design, an octagon with a slightly depressed center. The raised relief bulldog precludes its use as a trivet. We found two of these in the archives of the Ohio Museum of Ceramics. Cute though it is, I had decided to omit it from the book until we saw one in an antique shop, priced at $245!

This is a good example of the vagaries of setting prices. First of all, of course, the seller must make a profit, so part of the selling price is based upon what he paid. What the market will bear is determined by many factors. Scarcity, age, and condition obviously play a part, but so does geography -- where the piece is from and where it is sold. The popularity of the character illustrated or the business represented also influences the price. Apparently Webber's Ale & Beer of East Liverpool or bulldogs are popular in the area near the antique shop.

Premiums that continued to be popular into the '50s and later were those made for large corporations, like the Kelvinator jar. I had always assumed that the Campbell Kids, like Hopalong Cassidy and Buster Brown, could not appear on ware unless they had been licensed. Apparently, for a while this Campbell Kid was used freely.

Plate 39. Webber's Ale & Beer trivet, $245.00.

Plate 40. Boy and Dog plate, $15.00; Campbell Kid Plate, $22.00.

Then as now, people bought ceramics as gifts for family and friends. The "Mother" and "Dad" cups and saucers in Plate 41 are not backstamped, but they were made by Harker. The Hillbilly set and the Antique Auto set are part of many items produced for the gift trade. The plate in the center is from a convention of U.S. Postmasters that was held in Puerto Rico, and the Gadroon plate is from a letter carriers convention in Cincinnati.

Although the National Brotherhood of Operative Potters, the potters' union, had been recognized since 1912, after World War II the union label often became more important to consumers, so the letter carriers convention plate bears a Harker mark that includes the symbol and name of the union.

Most of the pottery in this chapter was made originally to advertise a business, to promote a tourist center, or to be sold as a gift. These purposes are usually short-term investments, but for a collector they can provide long-term delight and satisfaction.

HARKER CHINA CO.
EAST LIVERPOOL. OHIO

Fig. 14. Incorporating the union label is this monochrome stamp ca. 1959.

Plate 41. "Mother" and "Dad" sets, $10.00; Hillbilly and Antique Auto sets, $10.00; Letter Carriers Convention on left and Postmasters on right, $2.00-10.00.

──Chapter Five──
The Best of Times...The Worst

An atmosphere of "Anything Goes" began to stir during the late '20s. As the stock market seemed to promise that anyone could get rich, Americans began to demand a variety of household products, and a housewife with the most limited budget would be tempted by the dinnerware produced. Not even the Depression or World War II stopped the creative process significantly. And as the boys came marching home and the little woman returned from the factory, they bought new homes and new dinnerware.

The period of twenty years from the mid-'30s to the mid-'50s was the most creative for the potteries that produced American dinnerware. Why did a customarily conservative industry suddenly explode with dozens of new designs, products, and techniques? These years were not all pleasant times, conducive to creativity; perhaps it was the changes in America itself that were reflected in the exciting dinnerware and kitchenware produced in the Ohio Valley. Or perhaps it was the burst of light that precedes the death of a star, for the end of the American pottery industry was already in sight.

The East Liverpool potteries vied with one another to market the latest innovation in tableware, although there were both competition and cooperation among them. All copied one another's successful ideas, and all often used the same decals. Frequently they even "farmed out" contracts to each other, which is the reason that we sometimes find the same shape and decal with two different companies' backstamps. This Harker teapot and matching 6" plate with red and black lines on white are an exact match for a line by Homer Laughlin Pottery.

Helen Stiles wrote in 1941:

> If we start from Pittsburgh and follow the Ohio River until we cross the Pennsylvania line into that little corner of West Virginia which is sandwiched between Pennsylvania and Ohio, we will soon realize that we are approaching a pottery district. Wayside markets, one after another, present their colorful ware.... The quality is remarkable for the price we pay. We arrive in Chester, West Virginia, and perhaps visit...Harkers which is the oldest pottery in operation in this section.

In fact, Harker was the oldest pottery in operation in the United States at the time. The little town of Chester boasted other potteries, but Harker was the one that had its sign posted above the gas station at the foot of U.S. 30 boasting its age: "The Oldest Pottery in America/ Quality China since 1840/ The Harker Pottery Co./ One Piece or a Carload." Another famous landmark of the age, the Teapot, a wooden building that *Ripley's Believe It or Not* called "the world's biggest teapot," sold refreshments and ceramic souvenirs from all the local potteries to tourists who came to Rock Springs Park or were just passing through on U.S. 30.

In the competitive industry, potteries had to respond to public demand quickly or die. New shapes and decorating patterns replaced older ones that seemed a little stodgy to a younger generation. Paris, Melrose, and Embassy shapes were introduced throughout the late '20s and early '30s. Melrose preshadowed the squared-off lines of the Virginia blank which was to become popular later, but it kept the raised edge of Grandma's china. In bright, jazz-age colors, decals like Oriental Poppy and Tulips trimmed the line.

Plate 42. Both the teapot, $20.00, and the plate, $3.00, carry the Red Arrow mark.

Photograph 1. Photo courtesy of Mrs. Valma Baxter, whose husband Paul is pictured in front of the gas station. Mrs. Baxter worked for Harker Pottery from the time that it moved to Chester to its closing.

Photograph 2. This old postcard features the Teapot and its adjacent annex.

Plate 43. Melrose salad bowls, $9.00 each; cake lifter, $10.00; Arches mixing bowl, $20.00; Melrose platter, originally $25.00; Hi-Rise jug, $30.00, are in Oriental Poppy and bear a variety of marks.

Oriental Poppy is a good example of the illogical names given to decorations. The main flower in the decal is a large yellow chrysanthemum, and the orange-red flowers that surround it have only a passing resemblance to poppies. This pattern has also been called Poppy, and a promotional brochure ("Tear off the coupon and present it with your purchase to receive your free matching lipped and handled bowl! 34 pieces for $8.95!") called it American Beauty. Although we usually associate that name with roses, nary a rose is in the decal.

The two small bowls, in the Melrose shape in Plate 43, were part of a set of three nested salad bowls. The Melrose platter, shattered and reassembled, was big enough for the largest of Thanksgiving turkeys. The mixing bowl is in the Arches shape. The tall, rectangular jug in the photograph is often called Hi-Rise and was part of the movement toward modern angular lines and space-conserving shapes. The cake lifter is in Harker's standard shape.

Plate 44. G.C. custards, $4.00 each; pie baker, $15.00; syrup jug, $15.00, in Tulips carry several marks.

This decal in Plate 44 has had several names (Ruffled or Ragged Tulips), but Harker memos and sales brochures referred to it simply as Tulip. The custard cups are trimmed with the raised parallel lines in a chevron that mark the G.C. line, not a shape name itself, but an embellishment added to other shapes. The jug with a missing lid is part of a batter set.

Plate 45. Carnivale custards on Arches shape, $6.00; Anemones Virginia utility plate, $15.00; Anemones stackable, $7.00; Faded Carnivale 6" plate on Melrose shape, $2.00; Anemones spoon and cake lifter, $20.00; Carnivale Regal/Gargoyle pitcher, $25.00.

One of my favorites is the decoration I call Anemones. I don't know its real name, but the bright blossoms with their black centers remind me of wind flowers or gaily-colored balloons. The big Virginia platter sold with a lifter formed a cake set. The covered bowl is one of a set of two or more stackable storage jars. Sometimes a complete set can be found or assembled piece by piece. Serving spoons, lifters, and forks are popular with collectors. With a small mixing bowl, the fork and spoon form a salad set.

Carnivale is another interesting design from this era. Stylized flowers in bittersweet and yellow twine among green leaves and black stems and dots. The small Melrose plate has two backstamps: a bow and arrow with "1840" and the HotOven mark. The custards are molded in the Arches shape, and the jug is on Regal or Gargoyle (from the little figure on the handle.)

One shape reviewed in *China, Glass & Lamps* after the July 1938 Trade Show was called Newport: "designed on roundly curved lines with ball knobs and ring-shaped handles....Pastel tints of pink, blue, yellow, and turquoise green, used in single or double bands with handles and knobs of color." The cream and sugar set in Plate 46 are from the Newport line. Under the mark, the words "Celestial Blue," the color name, are stamped in gold.

Plate 46. Newport sugar and creamer with no lids are marked with the Open-Fletching Arrow and the color name. $5.00.

The same article described four new decorations: "Peasant, farm scenes in bright colors; Italian Rose, a bright-toned floral center; Hollyhock, a side spray in soft colors; and Tarrytown, a modern design in gray and red."

Embassy was a classical shape in keeping with Harker's policy of offering something for every taste. From "Showroom by Showroom as Seen by Madeline Love" in *China, Glass and Lamps* of February 1937:

> "Embassy," a new shape built along simple lines, with a wide rim, scroll handles, and acorn-shaped knobs...in a variety of designs ... Cornflower, ...red and gray bands, ...a clipper ship.

A clipper ship? Yes, but I've never seen it. Many decoration patterns are "lost" because they didn't sell well at the big trade shows held in January and July. We know they were produced in limited quantity for these shows because they were reviewed in trade journals. Unfortunately, we can only imagine the designs until they are found. But there is enough variety in the designs that survive to satisfy any collector. Elegant ivies and other vines, luscious fruits, and enough roses — Bridal Rose, Rosettes, Italian Rose, Margaret Rose, Rosebud, Rose Minuet, Rusty Rose, Royal Rose, Teal Rose, and Sweetheart Rose, not to mention three kinds of Petit Point Roses — to fill a cupboard all by themselves.

Plate 47. Embassy covered dish, $15.00, dinner plate, $5.00, and fruit dish, $1.00, with unknown decal.

Plate 48. Shadow Rose. Five treatments of the same decal on several different shapes: plain round, coupe, Virginia, and Gadroon. The Gadroon sugar and creamer set are marked Sweetheart Rose under the Royal Gadroon mark. The open sugar bowl is an unknown shape. $1.00-10.00.

Several of these roses, however, are different treatments of the same decal. A design that I call the Shadow Rose because it has a spray of pink and yellow roses with a light gray "shadow" was used almost a dozen different ways. In an all-over pattern that Jo Cunningham calls Rose Spray, it was supposedly made for the girls of the Harker family. The same decal was cut up and applied only on the edges of a plain round plate, either solid white or banded in ivory. A single spray was also centered on Royal Gadroon.

Plate 49. Shadow Rose. A Swirl shape vegetable bowl and Plain Round plate with Bridal Rose decals. I cannot document the name of the Rosebud Gadroon creamer. $1.00-10.00.

Teal Rose and Royal Rose are the same decal. The former was on the Aladdin shape brought out in the early '40s. Aladdin plates had ogee shoulders — a double curve that formed *S* in profile — and the teapot and creamer and sugar sets were suggestive of Aladdin's magic lamp. Even the shaker sets were unusual flattened shapes. The Royal Rose was the same decal used on the round Gadroon blank. The small lugged platter with the Slender Leaf pattern is also Aladdin shape.

Another classic design that many potteries tried was a laurel wreath. Harker called their version Laurelton, with the wreath around the rim of the plates wiped of some color to the highlight the design. I understand the Laurelton, made in several colors including teal, pink-cocoa, and gray, didn't sell well, but Harker used it later in the '60s as a blank for the Rockingham plates and trivets.

Lois Lehner said, "No doubt part of Harker's huge success for so many years was the fact that not only did the family stay with the business, but a line of faithful employees also stayed, giving the company a certain pride in their products." A close-knit organization, run by one family for generations and, in many cases, employing whole families of craftspeople, Harker was quickly responsive to new trends and ideas. If America wanted designs with American Indian influences, they got it. I have found two references to such patterns — Navajo and Wampum — but I have none in my collection.

Plate 50. Laurelton and Aladdin. Laurelton teal 7" plate, $3.00, and pink-cocoa cup and saucer, $6.00. Teal Rose on Aladdin plate, $8.00, and creamer, $5.00; Slender Leaf lugged plate, $8.00, and celadon Aladdin creamer, $5.00. All bear a variety of stamps.

Heritance began as a severely classical white on twelve-sided plates and hexagonal cups. Only a thin band of platinum adorned the edge. A 69-piece set sold in 1954 for $39.90. Then tiny roses were strewn across the center. A decal called Delft, which would appear again in the '60s on Stone China, created the next version. I have been told that many other variations were made, including a solid royal blue. Harker did little with deeper colors, and I would love to see it, but I have yet to find this treasure.

Plate 51. Heritance. Only the dinner plate, $5.00, and the fruit dish, $2.00, carry the Heritance mark. The others — a cupless saucer, $1.00, Delft decal 7" plate, $6.00, and Rosebud vegetable, $5.00 — carry several different ones. The divided vegetable dish, $5.00, was a very popular item in the '50s.

Fig. 15A   Fig. 15B   Fig. 15C   Fig. 15D   Fig. 15E

A variety of marks were used on ware of this period, several of which I cannot document. **Fig. 15A**. Monochrome ca. 1955-65. **Fig. 15B**. Monochrome ca. 1955-65. **Fig. 15C**. Monochrome No documented date. **Fig. 15D**. Monochrome ca. 1960-72. **Fig. 15E**. Top impressed, bottom monochrome. No documented date.

Plate 52. Pink and Charcoal. Mary on Virginia utility plate, $10.00; Erica oval lugged platter, $8.00; Donna cake plate and lifter, $20.00; and Pine Cone 6" coupe plate, $2.00, bear a variety of marks.

Plate 53. This Tulip Bouquet set is unusually large, having eight instead of the standard six serving plates. All are in the Virginia shape and carry the Open-Fletching Arrow in gold. $50.00.

Color was as important to the pottery industry as to the fashion industry. The fad for pink and gray that swept America in the '50s can be seen in home magazines of the era. Harker made several lines to meet the demand. The design which I call Mary on the Virginia utility platter was called Hal Harker's decal by the decorating department. The oval platter with curved lugs I call Erica, and the cake plate and lifter with their delicate design in pink, gray, and black I have named Donna. The black and white pine cone, however, is listed in Harker sales literature as Pine Cone.

Except for a few vases, Harker produced little in the way of art pottery, but housewives of the era gave and received pretty cake and party sets that the firm produced. The shape is called Virginia, and the decal has several names. I prefer to call it Tulip Bouquet.

The gold scrolling embellishment is unusually ornate for Harker, although the firm retained hand-decorations long after other plants switched to machine applications. The gold patterns were applied by hand with a rubber stamp. The decorator had to judge by eye alone the spacing and angle of application.

Gold and platinum (silver would tarnish) trim lines were also put on by hand. The craftspeople who did this were amazing to watch. Usually, the piece to be lined was placed on a circular wheel set on an adjustable base. The liner could rest his or her elbow, spin the wheel, and quickly edge a plate or cup. Sometimes, to show off, a decorator would place a plate on upturned fingertips and twirl it with a twist of the wrist while applying a perfect gold line.

The gold and platinum, suspended in a liquid medium, were too thinly applied to be recoverable from broken ware, but the brushes, wiping cloths, and other tools were collected and processed to salvage every grain.

During World War II, Harker upheld its reputation as a "family pottery" and a "good shop" by keeping in touch with the employees in uniform. Mimeographed newsletters, preserved in the archives of the Museum of Ceramics, gave what news was possible about the movements of those serving their country. Blood drives and rationing, all the civilian disciplines of those years are recorded too. When the war ended, some did not return to their places on the line, and the pottery mourned.

In 1947, Harker expanded, building four tunnel kilns and two decoration kilns, using the latest technology in anticipation of the better times everyone expected. In April 1951, a memo to Harker's employees boasted a "new high monthly record of shipments totaling $235,000 for March," and each department supervisor was given a souvenir plate to mark the occasion.

Nevertheless, the end was already in sight. Rising production and personnel costs, the increasing use of

Plate 54. $235,000 plate. From the collection of Paul Pinney. NFS.

plastics, and the abundance of cheaper imports were slowly strangling the smaller potteries. When concessions were made to Japan in the '50s to secure airbases in return for lower tariffs, David Boyce said that "it (the treaty) means pure death to the industry,"

22 KT. GOLD

Fig. 16A   **Fig. 16B**   **Fig. 16C**   **Fig. 16D**

1840 BOW AND ARROW, RED ARROW, AND OPEN-FLETCHING ARROW. **Fig. 16A**. Monochrome ca. 1930-45. General use. **Fig. 16B**. Monochrome ca. 1950. Called the Red Arrow by the Decorating Department because it was usually printed in red. General use. **Fig.16C**. Monochrome ca. 1950. General use. **Fig. 16D**. Gold ca. 1950. General use.

Chapter Six
Other Kitchens, Other Times

I am especially fond of my Harker mixing bowls, although few of them are in mint condition. They are scratched, the decals are faded, and the gold or platinum trim lines are almost gone, but I find something comforting in knowing that I am part of a chain, a sisterhood of women who mixed up bread and cookies and meatloaf in the same bowls. The big bowl with its green edge line and Cherry Blossom trim, in which I mix up bread dough, inspires me with confidence. Many such old bowls can be found with marks that predate the HotOven and Bakerite backstamps.

One of the first shapes for these bowls that were made before the oven-safe era was the Arches mold, also referred to as Ropes and Arches. The series of arcs molded into the sides was accented by a rope-like pattern above the arches.

It is an old idea copied from earlier English ware.

Advertised as the first decal-decorated ware that was oven-to-table safe, HotOven kitchenware was introduced by Harker in 1926, followed by Bakerite and SunGlow in 1935 and 1937 respectively. The original lines were brought out on older shapes — Melrose and Windsor — but later the ware was made primarily on the Zephyr shape, which became the most popular. Zephyr is characterized by a series of concentric steps on the base and lids and by spherical or wing-like finials.

Expanded into dinnerware as well as oven-safe cookware, HotOven, SunGlow, and Bakerite were decorated in a variety of floral and other popular designs. To add elegance, the edges were often lined with gold and platinum as well as hand-applied color accents.

Plate 55. Top: Lisa on Arches shape, $25.00; English Ivy on Zephyr, $20.00; Ivy on Arches, $10.00;. Bottom: Jessica on Zephyr, $25.00; Cherry Blossom, $40.00, and Gladiola, $15.00, on Arches. Most carry the 1840 Arrow mark.

Plate 56. I usually carry my camera on antique and collectible expeditions so that I can record interesting or unafford-able species. I spotted a beautiful bowl across a crowded room at an antique flea market. By the time I pushed my way to its side, it had been purchased by another enthusiast. She kindly consented to my photographing it. I call the pattern "Orange Blossoms." Isn't it lovely? So quickly did I photograph the bowl sitting on the dealer's table with his other wares that the price sticker wasn't removed, but I forgot to record the backstamp.

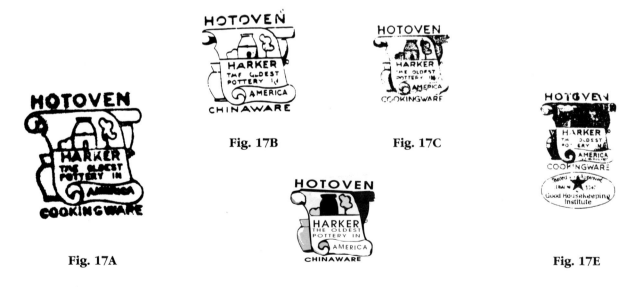

Hotoven dates from 1926, but most books of marks put the date at 1935. I believe that Harker probably used monochrome stamps originally and switched to color later. **Fig. 17A**. HotOven Cookingware - Monochrome ca. 1926-1950. **Fig. 17B**. HotOven Chinaware - Monochrome ca. 1926-1950. **Fig. 17C**. HotOven Cookingware - Color decal ca. 1935-1950. **Fig. 17D**. HotOven Chinaware - Color Decal 1935-1950. **Fig. 17E**. HotOven with Good Housekeeping Seal - Color decal ca. 1935-1950.

Fig. 18A   **Fig. 18B**   **Fig. 18C**

Bakerite was introduced after HotOven, but probably not by long. The two marks were used more or less simultaneously, but the gold mark was used longer. The OvenWare mark is one that I garnered from cuttings at the Ohio Museum of Ceramics, but I have never seen it used or been able to document it. **Fig. 18A.** Color ca. 1935. **Fig. 18B.** Gold ca. 1935-50. Found on both kitchenware and dinnerware. **Fig. 18C.** Undocumented.

What is the difference between HotOven, Bakerite, and SunGlow? The answer is "None." All these labels are on the same ware. It is possible to find the beloved Red Apple design on the Zephyr shape on a half-dozen different pieces with a half-dozen different marks.

Photos of my daughter Carla's collection, plate 57, 58, and 59, show some of the variations in decal and shape. Jo Cunningham has designated the smaller continuous design Red Apple I and the larger single design Red Apple II. In the first grouping, plate 57, the plates are all Virginia shape and the drips jar and shaker are Skyscraper. The second grouping, plate 58, shows the Zephyr shape bowls and teapot and a plain round plate. The third grouping, plate 59, contains Modern Age plate and shakers. The mixing bowl and custard are simple flared shapes, and the spherical sugar bowl is often referred to as part of the Zephyr line. Most of the pieces have the HotOven mark.

Why did Harker use so many marks? To meet the demands of the market. Retailers wanted "new" lines and "exclusive" markets. Harker gave them what they wanted through the simple expedient of changing the backstamps. If they used a new stamp, they suddenly had a new line. It was this same reasoning that created Columbia China in 1935.

Plate 57. Red Apple I on Virginia utility plate, $25.00; a batter jug, $20.00; and a saucer to a jumbo cup and saucer set, $5.00. Red Apple II on the center Virginia utility plate, $25.00; the Skyscraper drips jar, $15.00; the Virginia 6" plate, $5.00; and the Skyscraper salt shaker, $10.00.

Plate 58. Red Apple II on the Zephyr teapot, $30.00, and the plain round dinner plate, $10.00. Red Apple I on the small Zephyr utility bowl, $6.00; the open Zephyr bowl, $10.00; and the covered Zephyr bowl, $25.00.

Plate 59. Red Apple I on the mixing bowl, $20.00; Red Apple II on the Modern Age shakers, $20.00; the Modern Age cheese plate, $20.00; the G.C. custard, $8.00; and the spherical Zephyr sugar, $15.00.

Plate 60. Harker's HotOven sign. Ohio Museum of Ceramics. NFS.

One device used to promote HotOven in shows and ads was a colorful ceramic sign made in the shape of the HotOven mark, a scroll with a beehive kiln on it. It reminds me of the ceramic "calling card" pictured in Chapter 1 that Harker, Thompson & Co. used several generations earlier.

In order to appeal to the modern "deco" style, Harker brought out Modern Age shape -- a narrow oval shape usually decorated with a v-shaped pattern like the fletchings of an arrow -- in 1939. Designed for easy storage, the line boasted finials made like open circles or Life-Savers.

Originally, Modern Age, advertised in *China, Glass and Lamps* in December 1939 as the "Ware of Tomorrow," was a separate line with its own shape, its own embellishment, and its own decoration, primarily Modern Tulip with orange and brown stylized lines that suited the shape so well.

Plate 61. Modern Tulip on Modern Age. Top: Standard pie baker, $15.00; Zephyr utility cup, $8.00; Zephyr custard cup, $5.00; 6" plain round plate, $5.00; Modern Age creamer, $8.00. Bottom: Modern Age cookie jar, $35.00; Square water jug, $25.00; Modern Age teapot, $30.00. All in Modern Tulip and marked with Gold Bakerite.

Plate 62. Pastel Tulip casserole, $25.00, and Virginia dinner plate, $10.00. Pastel Posies Zephyr cheese bowl, $10.00, and Modern Age utility bowl, $10.00.

However, again to meet demand, Harker added the shape to other lines and used the Modern Tulip pattern on other shapes. One attractive idea that Harker marketed was a cheese tray set. The tray for crackers was usually a round Zephyr plate with its concentric circles. A small covered bowl, usually also in Zephyr and called an "individual casserole" or "cheese bowl," sat in the middle. Sometimes both pieces were plain or imprinted with the Modern Age embossed arrow.

I have found no name for the pastel posies decal on the cheese bowl and Zephyr utility bowl pictured in plate 62, so I call them just Pastel Posies. Pastel Tulips with its graceful tulips in soft violets, pinks, and greens is a more traditional design used by half a dozen manufacturers.

Fig. 19A

The v-shaped pattern of the arrow fletchings was used on both the mark and as an impression on the ware. **Fig. 19A**. Monochrome ca. 1939-47. **Fig. 19B**. Drawn from rubbing of design on ware.

Fig. 19B

Plate 63. Colonial Lady lugged soup, $8.00; 6" plate, $5.00; 8" embossed edge, $10.00; 9" Virginia dinner plates, $10.00; Cup and saucer, $8.00; footed bowl, $15.00; nappy, $10.00.

Colonial Lady, like Red Apple, seems to have been one of Harker's most endearing lines. In the '30s every pottery put out a silhouette pattern. This one — often confused with W.S. George's design — is supposed to have been particularly popular on Dish Night at movie theaters. Colonial Lady graces almost every shape Harker made: plain round, Virginia, Modern Age, Zephyr, and on a scalloped and embossed blank for which I have found no name. The spoon and casserole, the lid of which has a notch to accommodate the spoon, are a set. The utility bowl is called a "footed bowl."

Very close to Colonial Lady in design was a decal called Fireplace. In black and white with a similar square "window," an old-fashioned stone fireplace glows with a red fire. Above the flames a teakettle steams. I first saw it in Valma Baxter's log book, and two weeks later — too late to include in the book — I found a mixing bowl in an antique shop.

Plate 64. Three kinds of Colonial Lady jugs: an Arches mold, $25.00; Modern Age, $15.00; paneled syrup jug, $15.00. Two covered dishes: a slotted lid casserole, $25.00; au gratin, $20.00. The spoon, usually $10.00, is part of a set with the casserole.

Most potteries in this period put out their versions of a Mexican motif. As a teacher of Spanish for many years, I decorate my kitchen with these colorful designs. Harker put out two -- Monterey, in red, white, and blue on the Zephyr shape, and one I call Cactus for obvious reasons. The Monterey coffeepot has its original metal brewer. The Cactus rolling pin is flawed by a crack on the reverse side. For this reason, I got a bargain, but rolling pins normally are outrageously expensive.

Another popular decorative idea for kitchenware and dinnerware of the '30s and '40s was a picture of a cottage, a quaint one with flower gardens, smoke coming from the chimney, and a path to the door. Harker put out three, none of which, unfortunately, are pictured here: Doll House, Countryside, and English Countryside. All of these are pictured in Jo Cunningham's *Encyclopedia of American Dinnerware*. I have also found references to Cottage and Honeymoon Cottage in sources, but I suspect that these are alternate names for the same ware.

Plate 65. Top: Monterey Zephyr cheese tray, $30.00; coffeepot, $50.00; lunch plate, $6.00 and casserole, $25.00. Bottom: Cactus pie baker, $15.00; cracked rolling pin, $10.00 and Virginia utility plate, $15.00.

Many floral patterns were used on the HotOven, Bakerite, and Modern Age lines of cookware, tableware, and kitchenware -- bowls, casseroles, coffeepots and teapots, scoops, shakers and drip jars, rolling pins -- including Amy with its pink, peach, and white flowers; Mallow with its touch of black, and Pansy, which is often confused with Mallow. I wish I had a piece of Pansy to let you compare the two. This variety of shapes, patterns and items makes HotOven, Bakerite, and Modern Age increasingly popular with collectors, second only to Cameoware.

Amy is actually two decals. An older one, which was often called White Rose in the pottery, is seen on the casserole in Plate 66. Amy I had a white rose as its largest blossom. Amy II, seen on the other pieces, featured a white poppy instead. It is really difficult to see the difference without comparing the two side by side. Incidentally, I can find no documentation of the name Amy at all.

Plate 66. Amy dinner plate, $10.00; casserole, $25.00; unmarked and unknown 6" plate, $3.00. Bottom: Spoon, $10.00; dinner plate, $10.00; cake lifter, $10.00.

I can document neither the shape or decal name nor the use to which this brightly colored square casserole, in Plate 68, was put. I have been told that it was a salt keeper, and the stains that even several weeks of soaking in household bleach won't remove seem to indicate that it was used near the range. It is stamped with the multicolor HotOven decal. I call it Auntie Q after the shop where I found it.

Plate 68. Auntie Q square casserole, $12.00.

Plate 67. Mallow. Top: custard cup, $5.00; G.C. coffeepot, $25.00; paneled cream jug, $10.00. Bottom: Lipped bowl, $30.00 and mixing bowl, $25.00.

Plate 69. Deco Dahlia. Top: Skyscraper lard jar, $10.00; individual bean pot, $5.00; Virginia plate, $10.00; Au gratin casserole, $20.00; skyscraper shakers, $15.00. Bottom: Pie baker, $15.00; scoop, $6.00; handled utility mug, $15.00; Hi-Rise jug, $30.00.

Deco Dahlia, a stylized design in red and black or blue and black, has become very popular. In the decorating department, the patterns were called Red and Blue Daisies. The range set pictured illustrates Harker's traditional shape for shakers and drip jars called Skyscraper. The Skyscraper shakers were frequently sold to jobbers, and to add to the confusion, Harker rarely marked small items like this because the marks were hand-applied and thus costly. Also, I have even turned over one set to see "Made in Japan" marked on the base. The scoop is rare and often very expensive. I was lucky enough to find this one reasonably priced in a mission thrift shop.

Calico Tulip features the classic American color combination of red, white, and blue. The condiment jars with metal lids are the remnants of a set which included three to six jars and a wire rack.

Plate 70. Calico Tulip. G.C. condiment jars, $5.00 each, and Virginia utility plate, $20.00.

Plate 71. Ivy decal on D'Ware jar, $20.00; plain round plate, $10.00; spoon, $15.00; pie baker, $15.00 and round jug, $30.00.

One women's magazine of the '30s proclaimed Harker's Ivy as the perfect selection for a bride's casual dining and ovenware. My youngest daughter Corinne agrees, so I am assembling this collection for her. The oval lidded jar shape is called D'Ware, and the jug, which is missing a lid, was simply called a round jug. A teapot, seen in the next chapter, is from the Royal Gadroon line, a good example of Harker's practice of mixing shapes, lines, and patterns.

Sometimes it seems that everyone except me likes Petit Point, which the Harker decorators called Crosstitch. Jo Cunningham divides the variations into Petit Point I for the detailed design, Petit Point II for the less detailed, and Petit Point Rose for the rest. Because too many potteries used similar designs, Petit Point by any name is just another rose to me, but it is beloved by many other collectors.

China, Glass and Lamps in July 1937 proclaimed three new designs in Harker's ovenware and kitchenware:

"Petit Point" and "Tea for Two," the latter a pair of whistling teapots...[and] "Curiosity Shop" — a shelf of gay-tinted pottery.

Because Petit Point is so widely available and the other two are rare, I would trade my Petit Point for Tea for Two or Curiosity Shop any day.

Plate 72. A variety of the Petit Point decals. Top: Zephyr casserole, $25.00; octagonal tea trivet (one of Harker's traditional shapes), $10.00; Individual bean pot, $8.00; Zephyr coffeepot, $30.00. Bottom: Rolling pin, $85.00; Zephyr utility bowl, $8.00; mixing bowl, $25.00; spoon and fork, $20.00; plain round dinner plate, $10.00.

—Chapter Seven—
Variations on a Theme

Harker's Gadroon was perhaps its most versatile and, for the collector, most identifiable shape. The word *gadroon* refers to the rope-like pattern that decorates the edge of the plates. This scalloped decorative style has been used for centuries on many materials from china, glass, and wood to fabrics such as gadroon lace.

When searching through piles of plates at an antique store or a flea market, the collector can easily distinguish this edge from the plainer pieces in the pile. But beware! Harker sold thousands of these as blanks, either glazed or unglazed to jobbers, decorators, and even other potteries.

Because I am primarily interested in the Harker plant, I rarely buy any Gadroon ware that is not stamped with a Harker mark; I ignore the souvenir cups and plates, the church plates, ashtrays, and other ware without the Harker label. For someone looking for a specialty area, however, these items may be interesting. They are usually attractively priced, and many of the decorative patterns — photographs, decals, and hand-paintings — would make an attractive display. A collector could assemble a series of ashtrays, plates, or miniature cups and saucers from probably 48 states. Or collect church plates of a particular denomination. Or be limited only by the imagination.

Harker used several stamps and names for Gadroon dinnerware, but it can be divided into two groups: Chesterton, undecorated except for its rich colors and white edge, and the colorfully decorated Royal Gadroon.

The line usually called Chesterton was created by spraying the surface of the body (the basic clay shape) with colored glaze and then wiping the Gadroon embossing to produce an edging like white lace on the colored background. A 1949 memo gives credit to Jack McNicol, a Harker employee, for the idea.

Fig. 20A   **Fig. 20B**   **Fig. 20C**   **Fig. 20D**

Fig. 20A. Monochrome stamp. ca. 1950-60. Used primarily on silver gray Gadroon. **Fig. 20B**. Monochrome stamp. ca. 1948-55. Used on Gadroon and other shapes with raised edge. **Fig. 20C**. Monochrome stamp. ca. 1952-60. Used primarily on teal Gadroon. **Fig. 20D**. Impressed into raised oval. Used on a variety of ware, usually for export.

Plate 73. Chesterton Gray. Rear: Round Gadroon dinner plate, $8.00; Virginia Gadroon salad plate, $8.00. Front: Gadroon cup and saucer, $5.00; sugar bowl, $5.00; gravy boat, $8.00; creamer, $5.00; lugged soup/cereal bowl, $5.00.

Prim and elegant as a Quaker lady, silver-gray was produced first, so Chesterton is frequently used as the name of the color, the shape, and the line. The silver-gray and teal must have been particularly popular if one can judge by the services in shops and flea markets. A 93-piece service cost $57 in 1949, and today a collector can still build a lovely sevice in Chesterton for not much more.

The versatility of this shape is evident. Harker even produced charcoal/pink coffee and dessert sets to satisfy the late '50s rage for that combination, and a 1955 memo states that they intended to switch to the more "natural" combination of silver-gray and pink when the "pink and charcoal craze" ended. My service is gray, and I like to mix-and-match with pink-cocoa and yellow.

Plate 74. Corinthian. The place setting bears a variety of stamps. Rear: Gadroon cup and saucer, $5.00; Gadroon shallow soup, $5.00; Virginia Gadroon plate, $8.00; 6" plate, $5.00 and lugged soup/ceral bowl, $5.00. Front: Miniature cup and saucer often sold as a demitasse, $10.00; flat rimmed soup on round dinner plate, $8.00.

The collection here in Plates 74 and 75 I call Teal Chesterton, but it is also called Corinthian. All the pieces match, but the backstamps vary. Included are pieces marked Chesterton, Corinthian, and Pate-sur-Pate, as well as those marked with the Harker Square Cartouche. Some may even be marked with only an impressed Ironstone U.S.A. even though they are technically not ironstone.

Chesterton place settings commonly had three plates: a 9" and 10" Round Gadroon and an 8" Virginia Gadroon. The latter was sold primarily as a salad plate, dessert plate,

or — with a ring to hold the cup — a snack plate. These sets of plates and the matching cups were called Hostess Sets and were quite popular in the '50s as America became addicted to television and junk food. All Gadroon cups have a "dimpled" base.

The service pieces of the Chesterton line are also decorated with the gadroon. The pear-shaped shakers, elegantly curved gravy boats, creamers, and lidded sugars as well as the oval and round serving platters and dishes, were embellished with the rope-like pattern.

Plate 75. Corinthian cream and sugar set, $10.00; large oval platter, $15.00; gravy boat set, $8.00, on what was often sold as a pickle plate, $3.00; salt and pepper shakers, $6.00; round and oval vegetable bowls, $8.00 each.

Fig. 21A

Fig. 21B

Fig. 21A. Monochrome stamp used on chartreuse Gadroon. No documented dates. Photocopied from original ware. **Fig. 21B**. Monochrome stamp used on pale blue Gadroon. ca. 1955-65.

The Corinthian mark was used only on teal, and Sun Valley was used only on chartreuse. Some light blue Chesterton line was stamped Bermuda Blue/ Harker engobe ware. I have yet to find a special stamp on the Chesterton line in celadon (light sage green), charcoal, chocolate brown, coral, pink, pink-cocoa (pinkish beige), white, or yellow, but I will not be surprised when I find one.

Plate 76. A variety of colors and marks in the Gadroon shape. Top: Gray cup with pink interior, celadon, chocolate brown cup and saucer sets, $5.00 per set. Bottom: Plain white with two and one gold band, $2.00; pink cocoa, chartreuse, and teal 6" plates, $5.00. Charoal fruit dish, $3.00.

Plate 77. Celadon shakers, $6.00; yellow chop plate, $10.00; pink-cocoa Virginia plate, $8.00; pale blue tidbit tray, $6.00 and Bermuda Blue gravy boat, $8.00.

The yellow multiple-purpose plate pictured in Plate 77 was called a chop plate. The tidbit tray, marked with the Harker Square Cartouche, is a slightly different shade of blue from the gravy boat, which is stamped Bermuda Blue. I have noticed many variations in blues, and I am curious as to whether the differences are intentional or accidental.

The other use for the gadroon edge was to create the line called Royal Gadroon. Usually with a gold edge line and decorated with floral or other pretty decals, many of the Royal Gadroon family were marked with the decal name as well as the Harker stamp. In addition to Vintage and Violets, I have some marked Bridal Rose and Sweetheart Rose in my collection.

Because I could find no documentation of the mark, I have not included a copy of the "Royal Jackson" stamp that I have seen only in other books of marks. The mark, which was hand-drawn in the books, looks like the Royal Gadroon stamp, except that the word "Jackson" is substituted for "Gadroon." Just before we went to press, I was told by an authority, however, that Royal Jackson is an authentic mark.

Fig. 22A

Fig. 22B

Fig. 22C

Fig. 22D

Fig. 22A. Monochrome or gold stamp. ca. 1948-1963. Used on Gadroon decal ware. **Fig. 22B**. Gold stamp. ca. 1948. Used on Gadroon with Sweet Heart Rose decal. **Fig. 22C**. Gold stamp. ca. 1948. Used on Gadroon with Vintage decal. **Fig. 22D**. Multi-color decal. ca. 1948. Used on Gadroon.

Plate 78. Virginia gadroon dessert set, $10.00; embossed-edge cake plate and server, $30.00; Ivy on Teal cup and saucer, $10.00.

Dessert sets with an embossed floral edge were produced under the Chesterton and Pate-sur-Pate marks. The teal cake plate and lifter set pictured is one of these. But neither the Gadroon nor the embossed pattern is real pate-sur-pate. That process technically applies only to porcelain that is built up in layers by hand and then meticulously sculpted to detailed patterns. Harker simply used the name, I suppose, because it sounded elegant and because the embossed patterns were raised designs. I have found no name or documentation for the teal cup and saucer with the ivy on it, although I recently saw it on the Aladdin shape in an antique store. I call it Ivy on Teal.

Seven

Gadroon designs were used for complete services and specialty items. In addition to pretty, traditional patterns like Wild Rose, Violets, Ivy, Magnolia (sometimes called Springtime), and Vintage, some lovely stylized designs were made for the Gadroon blanks. One of my favorites is Bermuda, a circle of blue and gray leaves. I call the yellow and brown decal St. John's Wort because it reminds me of that wildflower, which grows in the meadows near our house. In Chapter 3 are examples of Bouquet and Ragwort. All of these were probably full lines that included all the serving accessories. I am not sure that Game Birds was a full line; I can't imagine an entire table covered with startled pheasants.

Plate 79. Top: Violets and Magnolia dinner plates, $8.00; Bermuda lunch plate, $5.00. Middle: Vintage platter, $11.00; St. John's Wort fruit dish, $3.00; Game Birds lunch plate, $5.00. Bottom: Wild Rose cake plate, $10.00; Vintage lugged soup/cereal bowl, $5.00; Ivy Vine Gadroon teapot, $30.00.

Plate 80. Top left and lower left: Godey chop plate, $10.00, and serving spoon, $10.00. Top right, middle, and lower right: Currier & Ives cake plate, $10.00; four assorted desserts, $5.00 each; and cake lifter, $10.00.

The Currier & Ives, Ivy, Vintage, and Godey — eighteenth century lovers — were popular patterns for eight-piece dessert sets that included a large (10") plate, six 6" dessert plates, and a cake lifter and sold for $4.50 in 1957. Godey has often been called Victorian Couple or George and Martha Washington. Until I came across the name Godey in Harker sales literature, I called them Eighteenth Century Lovers. I may be a hundred or so years off, but I know they are not Victorian, and I can't imagine George and Martha frolicking quite so carelessly. Another variation was the application of a thin coat glaze over the decal: Magnolia with a teal blush and Godey glazed with silver-gray.

The classic lines of the Gadroon made it adaptable. Many ashtrays, souvenir plates, and novelty items like the Antique Autos pictured in Plate 81 were produced. Thousands upon thousands of Gadroon ashtrays were sold as Americans puffed away and businesses advertised their products on the ever-present ashtray in those days before the designation of no-smoking areas. These attractive designs are among the last of the traditional decal-decorated ware from Harker. Although decals were added to Stone China and the Shellridge porcelain line in the '60s, neither displayed the variety or the charm of the Royal Gadroon.

Plate 81. Rear: Antique Auto cake plate, $10.00 and Virginia Gadroon plate, $8.00. Front: Antique Auto ashtrays in both Round Gadroon and coupe, $1.00-6.00.

—Chapter Eight—
Harker's Best

The ware that I and many others consider Harker's best was a patented intaglio process. The result was a design in white that seemed to be carved out of the colored surface. Often called "engobe" (pronounced "ahn-gobe" to rhyme with "globe"), the process is actually intaglio, which refers to a design that is carved into the surface. For years I called these designs "engobe," until I found out that the word means "colored slip" or liquid clay, the substance used to add color to many lines. Harker, by the way, usually referred to the area where this ware was made simply as "the color shed."

The process was brought over from Europe by German immigrant George Bauer. Bauer first worked in Baltimore, Maryland, at Bennett Pottery a descendant of the Bennett Brothers to whom Benjamin Harker Sr. once sold clay. Bennett apparently did very little with the process, and the company closed in 1936. When Bauer brought the idea to Harker, they began to use it on kitchenware and later on

Plate 82. One of several experimental designs that preceded the Dainty Flower. Gift from Paul Pinney. NFS.

dinnerware. Patented by Harker and originally produced in only blue on white, Cameoware was the trade name for the line that most books call Dainty Flower. In Harker sales literature and brochures the first pattern was called Dainty Blue or White Blossom. By any name, it was the result of a long, on-going experimental collaboration between Bauer and the Harker designers and workers. Later the intaglio production was expanded to include dozens of colors, decorations, and shapes.

The ware was originally produced by attaching a reverse stencil, the outline of the decoration desired, to the bisque body, clay that has been fired once. Then the bisque was dipped or sprayed with engobe, colored liquid clay. The rubber stencil was carefully removed with tweezers, washed, and reused. The piece was fired a second time to harden the engobe and then a third time after it was glazed.

This painstaking process could make detailed designs possible, but because worker error could blur the edges of the design and because the worker-intensive procedure was expensive, the results at first were disappointing and costs escalated. In my collection, I have several of these early experimental pieces, the patterns etched deeply into the engobe.

Continued experience brought change. The bisque was dipped or sprayed and then a true stencil — a mask with the desired decoration cut out — was placed over the body. With a grit under pressure, workers cut away the colored engobe. The resulting patterns were simpler, clearer, and to me, more pleasing. I like the later intaglio patterns much more than the Dainty Flower and White Rose.

Because the process involved several careful firings, Cameoware was originally guaranteed not to craze. As costs rose, however, shortcuts were taken; the engobe was applied to leather-hard rather than bisque body. The quality unfortunately suffered because the layers dried at different rates and this caused crazing.

Plate 83. Dainty Flower on Virginia and Skyscraper. Top: Virginia 6" plate, $5.00; Virginia utility plate, $20.00; Stained Skyscraper shakers, $6.00; Virginia fruit dish, $5.00. Bottom: Virginia vegetable bowl, $20.00.

But Cameoware was a success from the start. Advertised and featured in national magazines, the true-blue ware with its etched white pattern captured many hearts. It was chosen as the exclusive dinnerware and kitchenware line for the "Home of the Century" exhibit at Atlantic City's Steel Pier. Du Pont, who manufactured the engobe, used Cameoware to promote its ceramic colors line.

Today's collector can find Dainty Flower on almost every shape Harker ever made: plain round, Swirl, and Virginia flatware. The Swirl shape was marketed under the name Shellware. Most hollow ware is on Zephyr, but other, older shapes were used for smaller pieces like shakers. Harker even turned the big Virginia utility plate into a basket by adding a metal clip-on handle.

Always open to experimentation, Harker produced a line called Delft that was simply half white and half blue. The only intaglio used was to etch "S," "P," and "Drips" on the range set. To keep areas solid white, the bisque was covered with wax to resist the engobe. Special salad sets in blue on the Swirl shape with Pear or Tulip design were sold as gift sets.

Fig. 23A   Fig. 23A   Fig. 23A

Fig. 23A. Monochrome. ca. 1935-48 (Gates 1940-48.) Used primarily on dinnerware. **Fig. 23B**. Monochrome. ca. 1940-48. Used on dinnerware and kitchenware. **Fig. 23C**. Monochrome. ca. 1943. Used on dinnerware.

Plate 84. Dainty Flower on Swirl and Zephyr. Ashtray, $5.00; lunch plate, $10.00 and damaged Zephyr cookie jar, $25.00. Pear vegetable bowl is also in Swirl, $8.00.

Dainty Flower was soon etched into pink and yellow. Neither was as popular as the blue, then or today, but because less pink and especially less yellow were produced, their prices today are often much higher than other intaglios. The teal D'Ware shakers pictured are truly unusual because few dark colors were used for the intaglio design.

Plate 85. Yellow D'Ware shakers, $16.00; round jug, $30.00. Pink Virginia rectangular platter, $15.00. Teal D'Ware shakers, $25.00.

Boxed and sold as a unit, "Kiddo Sets," intaglio children's ware in traditional pink and blue, were made up of a cup, plate, and bowl. Hot water dishes were produced in both round and diamond shape, which is marked only "Glazed Inside" impressed in the base. Unfortunately the patterns were slightly garbled, the ducks almost indistinguishable from the umbrellas. The designs are so blurred that I have seen publicity photos where a display was upside down and nobody noticed!

Plate 86. Baby plate, $24.00, is from the collection of Mr. and Mrs. William A. Tighe. Kiddo set mugs, $20.00 each.

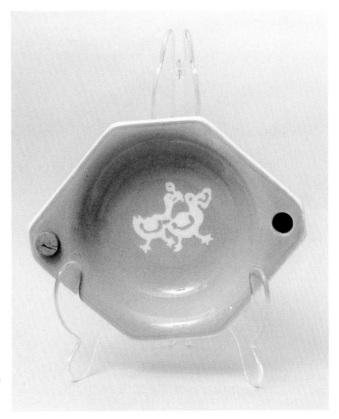

Plate 87. Early hot-water baby dish. Ohio Museum of Ceramics. $25.00.

White Rose was made exclusively for Montgomery Ward and was marked "Carv-Kraft" to avoid the use of the word "Cameo," which was patented by Harker. "Cameo Rose," used frequently by collectors, dealers, and writers, is a misnomer; neither Dainty Flower nor White Rose was called Cameo Rose by Harker. They did make an intaglio rose complete with stem and thorns under its own mark, but it was called merely Rose.

Harker produced ware, much of which does not carry the Harker name, for many large retailers. Among those easily found in flea markets and antique shops are Kelvinator refrigerator bowls, Montgomery-Ward's White Rose, and several lines for Sears Roebuck's Harmony House dinnerware. One delicate floral intaglio on pale blue engobe, Blue Rhythm, is the only intaglio on the Gadroon blank that I have found, and the abstract Egyptian pattern on the Heritance shape was called Lotus. Both were made for Sears' Harmony House.

Plate 88. Lotus dinner plate, $8.00; Rose platter, $14.00; Blue Rhythm dinner plate, $10.00; White Rose 6" plate, $5.00 and utility bowl, $8.00.

Fig. 24A.

Fig. 24B.

Fig. 24A. Monochrome. ca. 1940. Used only on Montgomery-Ward White Rose line. **Fig. 24B**. Monochrome. ca. 1950. Used with changes of catalog numbers and colors for various designs made for Sears.

Plate 89. Top: Ivy Wreath platter, $14.00; cream and sugar set, $20.00 and dinner plate, $10.00. Bottom: Vine Lace dinner, $10.00, lunch, $8.00, and 6" plates, $5.00; cup and saucer set, $10.00 and fruit, $5.00. Divided vegetable dish, $5.00, has no intaglio design.

Other colors and many other designs were soon added to the intaglio lines on the Olympic shape, a rolled-edge coupe (having no flat rim) with cups shaped like half an hour-glass, oval coupe soup bowls, and platters that were almost rectangular. Celadon green engobe etched with an ivy design and a wide white border was named Vine Lace. Without the border, it was labeled Ivy Wreath. Both were well liked then and now.

Another design on green was one that I have named Persian Key. Harker called the Pennsylvania Dutch design on the platter and cup either Provincial or Provincial Tulip. The ring of leaves, an unnamed pattern, is one variation of a design that was also used on blue (called Snow Leaf) and gray (called Coronet) and perhaps on other colors as well.

A variety of other designs, which I cannot document, are listed in books, memos, and sales literature. Because Harker was a close-knit "family shop," experimentation was encouraged. The variety of bodies, patterns, and intaglio combinations could have been even greater if the pottery industry had not been threatened by rising costs and shrinking markets. The intaglio process was expensive, and Harker had always been labor-intensive, using hand-dipping, hand-applied decals, and hand-lining after most potteries had gone to machines. No wonder one management memo pointed out that 60% of every dollar made went to salaries.

Plate 90. Provincial Tulip platter, $14.00, and cup and saucer set, $10.00; celadon Coronet lunch plate, $8.00; Persian Key lunch plate, $8.00.

Plate 91. Springtime dinner plate, $10.00; Dogwood lunch plate, $8.00; Rocaille dinner plate (broken and reassembled) $0 and cup and saucer, $10.00; Wheat platter, $14.00; Alpine 6" plate, $5.00 and Everglades dinner plate, $10.00.

Pink-cocoa is a rose-beige that produced handsome designs. Alpine is a white spray with a turquoise accent. Bamboo is obviously bamboo, Wheat is a cluster of cereal stalks, and Dogwood is unmistakable, but Harker called a design of cattails Everglades or Meadow Marsh if it had the Harmony House label. The old name Rocaille was resurrected for a pattern of scrollwork seen on a plate and cup. Springtime is a spray of meadow flowers and grass.

Coral is a much deeper shade than pink-cocoa. This coral platter design is called Cock O'Morn, and the tidbit tray is Country Cousins.

Plate 92. Country Cousins tidbit tray, $6.00, and Cock O'Morn platter, $14.00.

Yellow engobe inspired several daisy designs. With brown centers, white daisies on yellow are Black-eyed or Brown-eyed Susan. Without the tiny drops of brown engobe — which, incidentally, added to the cost of the line — the pattern is White Daisy. The white daisies in Daisy Lane had turquoise centers. Harker also listed a line called Daisy Dance. I don't know if it is simply another name for one of these or a variation like the white daisies with brown centers on pink-cocoa that I have seen.

Cock O'Morn on yellow became simply Rooster. Viking had a series of white diamonds on yellow and Sun-Glow was a burst of white rays on a gold tone. For Spanish Gold, designed by Paul Pinney, supervisor of the color shed, a gold engobe was edged with a blush of coral, producing a flaming sun, and then the intaglio pattern of leaves was etched.

I have no example of Star-Lite, an all-over pattern of starbursts on pale blue. On blue, a circle of abstract leaves was Snowleaf, and a ring of simple posies was Petit Fleurs. The intaglio cup is a variation of Springtime, which is usually on pink-cocoa.

Plate 93. Top: Sun-Glow dinner plate, $10.00; plain yellow cake lifter, $10.00. Middle: White Daisy dinner plate, $10.00; white and yellow cup, $5.00; Rooster tidbit tray, $6.00; Black-eyed Susan dinner plate, $10.00. Bottom: Spanish Gold lunch plate, $25.00; Black-eyed Susan three-tier tidbit tray, $12.00, and cup and saucer set, $10.00.

Plate 94. Oval soup/cereal bowl, $5.00; white and blue cup, $5.00; Petit Fleurs dinner plate, $10.00; Snowleaf lunch plate, $8.00; blue Springtime cup and saucer, $10.00.

Lois Lehner called the Cameo lines "another great collectible." Because they are unique, the intaglios are perhaps the most collectible of Harker ware. I try to find all the variations I can. I had been looking for an unknown pattern called Wild Rice, expecting it to be the usual centered design. While we were photographing material from the archives of the Ohio Museum of Ceramics, I found this small bowl -- Wild Rice at last! -- in a cupboard in the basement of the museum.

Plate 95. Wild Rice custard, $10.00. Ohio Museum of Ceramics.

Fig. 25A

Wild Rice
INTAGLIO
by
HARKER POTTERY CO
U.S.A.

Fig. 25B

Fig. 25A. Impressed. ca. 1954-65. Used on serving pieces in intaglio line as well as other lines. Fig. 25B. Monochrome. ca. 1950. Wild Rice line.

Paul Pinney began with Harker in 1940 and, except for service time during World War II, stayed with Harker until their closing. Paul, who was the supervisor of the color shed where Cameo and other intaglio were produced, has shown me experimental and limited production pieces, several of which he designed. Any pottery lover would cherish these unique items.

In one experiment, the body was dipped first in Corinthian, a dark teal, cut with a wreath of grapes and leaves, and then dipped again in Honey Brown. The pattern called Grapes on Teal glows like burnished bronze against a deep, dark background. Elegant with amber glassware! Unfortunately, Harker by this time was fighting a losing battle against plastics, imports, and rising costs, and many of these experiments were never produced in collectible numbers.

Plate 96. Grapes on Teal Paul's original design, NFS, is on the right, and the production version, $15.00, on the left. From the collection of Paul Pinney.

Not all experiments were sanctioned. My father-in-law made baby sets for my two older daughters in the early '60s. Such items are sometimes called "gypsy ware" because they were frequently made unofficially to sell for the worker's profit, often along the road.

The two trivets that we recently found were probably not released for sale. Remember Pearl Harbor with its airplane, sinking ship, harbor and palm trees, and I Love America were the products of local patriots in the '40s.

Plate 97. Patriotic trivets, $20.00 each; Baby Carla set, NFS.

HARKERWARE
by Russel Wright

Fig. 26. Impressed and incised mark of Russel Wright's lines for Harker Pottery. ca. 1953-55.

One group of intaglio is of interest to collectors who otherwise are unfamiliar with Harker. In the '50s famous industrial designer Russel Wright created his first patterned dinnerware line for Harker Pottery: White Clover, which won a good design competition held by the Museum of Modern Art.

The small florets and leaves of White Clover are etched into four decorator colors: Meadow Green, Coral Sand, Golden Spice, and Charcoal, but not all pieces have the clover design. I prefer the green, but the coral is considered the most collectible because less of it was produced. In 1954 a 16-piece set cost $9.95, except in California, where it cost $10.95 .

As with all Russel Wright designs, the stoneware bodies are gracefully "modern," spare but gently curved. The edge of the plates curls up sharply, and the bowls are irregular ovals. Most interesting are the shakers. Following the logic that people use more salt than pepper, Wright designed the salt twice as large as the pepper. In later lines like Tahiti, Harker used the larger salt shaker mold, but resisted using the original pepper. I suppose that the shakers were confusing to consumers; I have seen the sets mismatched -- two peppers or two salts -- in shops today.

Wright also designed a clock for Harker with a General Electric movement that sold for $8.98. A round-cornered square, the clock has raised numerals and was produced in the same colors as White Clover. Again, the coral is rarest. Clocks with the original movement are also more difficult to find and therefore more expensive. My own, the gold one pictured, had no movement or hands and cost $24. My husband put in works from a hobby shop.

Plate 98. Rear: Golden Spice Russel Wright clock, $24.00, and Charcoal White Clover dinner plate, $10.00. Front: Meadow Green White Clover utility bowl, $3.00, and cup, $5.00, Golden Spice shakers, $5.00. The ashtray, $6.00, is an experiment in color by Russel Wright.

The coral clock pictured illustrates the unpredictability of prices and of definitions of the word "mint." In coral, considered the "most collectible" color and with the original General Electric movement in working condition, this clock was reduced to $10 because of the chip at the top. A collector who is willing to live with minor flaws can find bargains.

The public's growing interest in functional design and their more casual lifestyles were the reasons for the popularity of Stone China in the '50s and '60s. The line of heavy gray stone china dipped in solid-color pastels and white (advertised as "*House & Garden* approved colors") became an instant success. They were guaranteed for a year against breakage or chipping.

The engobes contained tiny chips of metal that gave a peppered look to the colors and also irritated workers' hands. The edges of the pieces were wiped of color to provide a contrasting border. To prevent bubbling of the top surface engobe, the base of the body had to be cleaned by hand of all glaze. This added to the cost, but made the unglazed bases perfect knife sharpeners.

Plate 99. Russel Wright Clock, $10.00.

Plate 100. Stone China. Top: Blue Mist shaker set, $10.00; Golden Dawn platter, $6.00, cup and saucer set, $5.00; 6" plate, $2.00; Blue Mist oil and vinegar cruets, $10.00. Bottom: Blue Mist three-tier tidbit, $6.00, and cream and sugar set, $14.00; table setting of Blue Mist dinner plate, $6.00; Shell Pink salad plate, $2.00; Golden Dawn soup/cereal bowl, $2.00; three-tier tidbit tray in Shell Pink, Blue Mist, and White Cap or White Pepper, $6.00.

| **Fig. 27A**. | **Fig. 27B**. | **Fig. 27C**. |

Fig. 27A. Impressed mark. ca. 1954-72. Used on Stone China. **Fig. 27B**. Impressed mark. ca. 1954-72. Used on Stone China. Both drawn from original ware. **Fig. 27C**. Monochrome. ca. 1950-60. Used on Stone China.

| **Fig. 28A**. | **Fig. 28A**. |

Fig. 28A. Monochrome. **Fig. 28B**. Monochrome. ca. 1950. Used on decal-decorated Stone China.

So popular was Stone China that designs in colored engobe were soon added. Sea Fare, a free-hand design in color on white, reminds us of a fish. The covered soup bowl is unusual. Another lovely design was Trinidad, with full-blown pastel flowers; unfortunately, I have none of it to show you.

Soon someone tried the intaglio process on Stone China. Peacock or Peacock Alley was the result. Then came the tree pattern and several others. If the dots on the tree were yellow, it was called Lemon Tree. If they were gold, Orange Tree. I have no idea what strange fruit is growing on my plate, so I call it Forbidden Fruit.

A line of decal-decorated Stone China was produced under the backstamp of Country Style U.S.A. and Colonial, U.S.A. These brightly-colored patterns on gray won the Altman Award in 1958 sponsored by Altman's, the New York department store, "for fine tableware design in earthenware."

Stone China continued to be popular even after the Harker Pottery was sold to Jeanette Glass in 1969. Many of the patterns used on the ware in those latter days were produced by using stamps: giant rubber stamps that were made in the pottery. A thin rubber sheet with the desired design was bought from a manufacturer. At the pottery, the sheet was trimmed, glued to a frame of wood and foam rubber, and then adjusted to fit various sizes of bisque ware. The pattern was applied by a machine to the ware until the stamp wore down and then replaced. I have no examples of this ware.

What was Harker's best? In my opinion, the intaglio designs (including but not restricted to Dainty Flower), the Russel Wright line, and the early Stone China were the finest modern ware to bear the Harker mark. They were unique, not merely one of many imitations produced by dozens of potteries. This does not mean, of course, that they are necessarily the most avidly collected, although Dainty Flower continues to hold its own in the collectibles market.

Plate 101. Country Style and Colonial stoneware. Peacock dinner plate, $5.00; water jug, $25.00; and cup and saucer, $5.00. Provincial Wreath dinner plate, $5.00; Sea Fare covered soup cup and saucer, $10.00; Forbidden Fruit dinner plate, $5.00.

—Chapter Nine—
Back to the Roots

By the '60s, most of the leaders of the pottery industry knew that an era was over. Memos issued within Harker's walls and newspaper interviews of the period make it clear in retrospect that small potteries could not survive and that only conglomerates with their tax-loss incentives could continue production. Cold War treaties that traded tariffs for air bases were the last blow. A family business with its paternal consideration for employees could not survive against cheap-labor imports.

Harker tried desperately to hold on. One idea that collectors are glad that Harker tried was the revival of Rockingham ware. Designer Norman Clewlow was asked to model designs for the hound-handled pitcher that won Harker, Taylor and Company a gold medal over a century before.

Denied permission to handle or use the originals, Clewlow spent long hours in the Ohio Historical Society Museum of Ceramics studying the graceful jug through glass windows. Then he would go back to his studio and, from his sketches, model the clay. His success is undeniable. Some experts may declare the reproductions of the pitcher and the other pieces in the line as "uncollectible," but I have yet to meet a anyone who doesn't respond to the lines, detail, and color, a rich dark brown with a dribble effect in foamy white.

According to the same experts, only the green reproductions are worth collecting because, I presume, they do not imitate the originals. In Plate 104 are two reproduction jugs side by side, one green and one brown. Judge for yourself.

In addition to the jug, Harker produced matching hound-handled mugs, some with candleholder inserts. Then they added a Rebekah-at-the-Well teapot, originated in East Liverpool by James Bennett, according to E.W. Barber. Most of the Rebekah reproduction teapots that I have seen are plain brown, but I have seen one in bottle green.

Toby mugs in the form of Daniel Boone -- with a coonskin cap and a tree handle behind which an "Injun" hovers -- sold originally in the '60s for $2.95, but now command $20 to $150. Another toby mug called Jolly Roger, a pirate whose pigtail forms the handle, seems to be less popular if one judges by the prices.

These relatively inexpensive gift shop items included a soap dish, marked appropriately "SOAP," and an oval bread plate, a duplicate of an earlier design. The edge of the plate spells out "Give us this day our daily bread." The line also included plates and plaques with the American eagle seal on the Laurelton blank and on Harker's traditional octagonal trivet.

One bank in Chester has these Rockingham reproductions and several ashtrays in the shape of a tobacco leaf in the lobby. When I offered to buy one, the manager of the bank declined because Robert Boyce had placed them in the bank when he was president and had requested that they not be removed. When I asked to photograph them for reference, the manager obliged cheerfully, but the customers in the bank that day were a little puzzled.

Plates 102 and 103. An original Harker, Taylor and Co. jug from the Ohio Museum of Ceramics, $600.00, is above and a Rockingham Reproduction from the collection of Nancy Sabo, $50.00, on the right. More than the glaze was changed. The grape vines of the original were replaced by larger, simpler floral reliefs. The design of the base is also less detailed in the reproduction than in the original.

Plate 104 From the collection of Nancy Sabo of Pleasant Grove, Ohio. $50.00 each.

Plate 105. Top: Hound-handled mug, $25.00; Rebekah-at-the-Well teapot, $30.00 and Daniel Boone mug, $20.00. The teapot has no texture glaze. Bottom: Jolly Roger, $5.00, and Soap dish, $20.00, in Honey Brown; American Eagle plate on Laurelton blank, $8.00, and Jolly Roger in Bottle Green, $10.00.

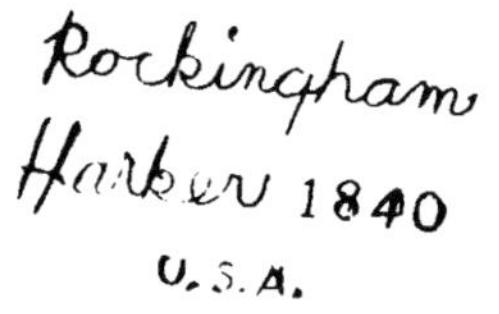

Rockingham Harker 1840 U.S.A.

Fig. 29A

Reproduction Harker Rockingham Mfg. 1848 U.S.A.

Fig. 29C

HARKER 1840
ANTIQUE REPRODUCTION
U.S.A.

Fig. 29D

Rockingham Harker U.S.A.

Fig. 29B

Rockingham HARKER 1840 U.S.A.

Fig. 29E

Fig. 29A. Impressed. ca. 1965. **Fig. 29B**. Impressed. ca. 1965. **Fig. 29C**. Impressed. ca. 1965. Note the discrepancy in the date of Harker's founding. **Fig. 29D**. Impressed. ca. 1965. **Fig. 29E**. Monochrome. ca. 1965.

The last stamp above (Fig. 29 E) had a variation that may be of interest for those who remember Rock Springs Park in Chester, West Virginia, and collect its memorabilia. We have seen some Rockingham pieces marked "Rock Springs Park" in the same script and obviously from the Harker plant. They must have been some of the last souvenirs sold before the park disappeared under U.S. 30.

I have also seen the reproductions, especially those that carry marks with the date but without the word "reproduction" selling for prices that almost match those of real antiques. Even the prices of those clearly marked as reproductions are rising.

Amusingly enough, there are copies of the copies! When Harker was sold to Jeanette Corporation in 1969, their molds, of course, were part of the deal. Some employees did not want to let anyone else make the Rockingham Reproductions of which they were so proud. One man went so far as to try to hide the molds in his basement, but the laws of commerce prevailed and the molds were sent to another acquisition of Jeanette. There more reproductions were made under a Royal Rockingham mark. The pieces are not so well made; the glaze is mottled and rough. Reportedly, some of the molds are in private hands today.

Plate 106. Royal Rockingham jug, $20.00, and mug, $10.00. The photo does not show the irregularity of the glaze.

Royal Rockingham Reproduction USA

Fig. 30. Impressed. Used after 1969.

Most potters did not like the drip effect used on the Rockingham Reproductions. Neither did my father-in-law, who dipped much of the ware, care for the line called Rawhide and sold under the stamp Quaker Maid. The shape pleased him, but to deliberately "ruin" a good glaze with "mistakes" offended his professional pride. However, the dark brown color with its drip effect must have pleased many others, for it sold well. McCoy's and Hull's versions are abundantly available to the collector, but Harker's is more difficult to find. Much of it was marketed under Pearl China's stamp, with the Ironstone USA impressed mark, or without any mark at all.

Plate 107. Rawhide or Quaker Maid. These pieces carry a variety of marks. The only reason that I know the big bowl is from Harker is that my father-in-law gave it to me. Top: Dinner plate, $5.00; cup and saucer, $5.00; fruit dish, $2.00, and creamer, $5.00. Bottom: Individual bean pot, $8.00; giant salad bowl, $10.00; utility bowl, $8.00.

Plate 108. $10.00. The glaze and color of this unstamped cream and sugar set is typically Harker, but the shape is wrong. I cannot imagine my father-in-law dipping these dainty feminine handles and finials in Rawhide's masculine browns. They may be Harker's, but I doubt it.

Fig. 31.

Fig. 32.

Fig. 31. Monochrome. ca. 1962. **Fig. 32.** Monochrome. ca. 1965. **Fig. 33.** The only documented mark for Rawhide was this Quaker Maid stamp. Because Harker made this ware for Pearl China, the word Pearl often replaces Harker on the mark. Most of this ware is unmarked or has the impressed Ironstone USA mark. Monochrome. ca. 1965.

Fig. 33.

Trying desperately to keep the pottery alive, the Boyce family tried several innovations. One of the most creative was the line called Wood Song. Modeled on the maple leaves, twigs, and seed pods that fill the Ohio Valley, Wood Song reportedly had "real leaves ... actually impregnated into unfired clay." This was undoubtedly advertising rhetoric, but a careful examination leads to admiration of the careful reproduction of shape and detail. I have no doubt that the modelers worked from real leaves, twigs, and seed pods. The handles and finials are authentically twig-like and the leaves and seeds are miniature replicas of those in my yard. Glazed in honey brown, bottle green, gray, and dark brown, Wood Song has not yet appeared in great numbers in the collectibles market, but because it was produced for only a short time, the persistent collector can unearth true rarities.

Many of the smaller pieces are not stamped, but anyone seeing Wood Song will have no trouble differentiating between it and Steubenville's more colorful but less realistic Woodfield.

Plate 109. Wood Song. Tea cup and saucer, $10.00; cream and sugar set, $15.00; fruit dish, $5.00; and coffee mug, $5.00 in Honey Brown. Butter dish in Sherwood Green, $8.00.

Undoubtedly the most complicated and expensive of Harker's later ware to produce was the line called Tahiti. Designed by Douglas Manning, Tahiti included shapes from several lines, including a shaker set based on Russel Wright's shaker. Dippers used teal as an undercoat and then masked and blasted an intaglio design of leaves and stems. The piece was dipped a second time in honey brown, producing deep green-bronze tones under dark brown. Then details were added by hand in several colors of engobe. The pattern of exotic leaves and flowers in green, blue, rose and cream on the dark background is not to the taste of those who prefer brighter, more traditional designs. One of my daughters dubbed it on first sight as "the world's ugliest Harker," and the unfortunate epithet stuck.

Frankly, Tahiti is an acquired taste, a sophisticated, unusual design. Unfortunately, it was also an expensive one, too labor-intensive to be profitable. But at least Tahiti went into production; some other experimental lines never saw even the lights of the showroom.

Plate 110. Tahiti shakers are modeled on Russel Wright salt shaker, $8.00. Ashtray, $5.00.

One line that was held an honored place in the Harker spotlight was Shellridge. I remember clearly how proud my new in-laws were of the Shellridge Leaf Swirl porcelain set that they gave my husband and me as a wedding gift. I was commanded to hold it to the light with my hand behind to see the shadow and to flick the edge with my fingernail to hear the ring. Shellridge was Harker's last attempt at decal-decorated dinner ware, but it was a lovely one. The shape itself is delicate as a seashell with striations much like a shell. The decals are elegantly understated in design and color.

Stainless flatware and glassware by leading manufacturers were created to match the Shellridge line, but I have been unable to find any pictures, names, or examples on the market.

In his Christmas message to the employees in 1960, David Boyce had little good news, but ended on a note of optimism:

Merry Christmas...Once again we have had a profitless year, filled with hard work, frustrations and difficult problems.... No dividends have been paid to Harker stock-holders during [the past five years]....sizeable expenditures...borrowed...increase in...state unempoyment ... social security taxes... gas, fuel, and maintenance costs...[and] labor costs....We sincerely believe that better days are just ahead.

Long before the pottery was sold to Jeanette Glass in 1969, the factory tried to diversify, producing "vitreous china plumbing fixtures": sinks and toilets. In a memo issued in April 1956, Robert E. Boyce insisted, "We have not given up on dinnerware." One authority remarked that anyone who can make a good bathtub can make good dinnerware. Perhaps so, but I thought it sad to find at the Ohio Museum of Ceramics this sales handout among those for the lovely table and ovenware that Harker made in 131 years of continuous operation.

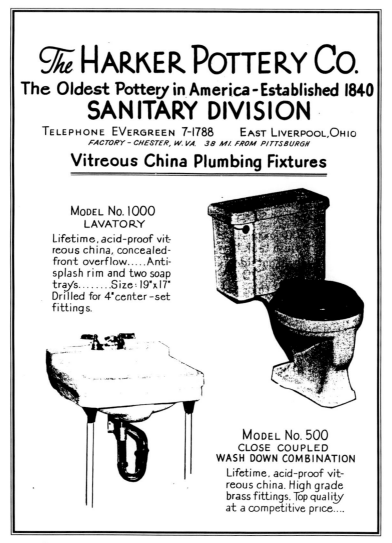

Fig. 35.

Whitechapel

TRANSLUCENT

THERMOWARE

U. S. A.

HARKER CHINA CO.

EAST LIVERPOOL

OHIO

Fig. 34A.   **Fig. 34B.**   **Fig. 34C.**

Fig. 34A. Monochrome. ca. 1960-72. Used primarily on Shellridge. **Fig 34B**. Monochrome or gold. ca. 1960-72. Used on Shellridge and other semi-porcelain like ashtrays. **Fig. 34C**. Monochrome. ca. 1960. Used on semi-porcelain and, according to some sources, white Gadroon.

Harker Pottery closed in 1972. The plant was used by Ohio Valley Stoneware for a few years, but in September 1975 the building burned down, lighting the night skies of East Liverpool and Chester with burst of red and orange flames and pillars of black smoke. Only the chimney with "Harker" spelled vertically down the side remains visible from the higher hills and the Jennings Randolph Bridge, and a warehouse built nearby still refers to the area as the "Harker dock."

Plate 111. Shellridge. The gravy boat, $20.00, is undecorated and unmarked, a gift from Paul Pinney. The 6" plate, $5.00, has a Forest Flower decal.

Plate 112. Harker chimney: all that is left of the pottery.

Today, a few blocks away, the World's Largest Teapot has been restored by the citizens of Chester and placed on a concrete pad below the bridge. Beehive kilns still stand, one in East Liverpool between U.S. 30 and the Ohio River and one at the north end of Wellsville, Ohio, just a few miles south. Many oldtimers in Chester or East Liverpool remember working at Harker's or one of the other defunct plants. Two large and several smaller specialty potteries remain in the area, and the Ohio Historical Society's Museum of Ceramics in East Liverpool preserves the memories of the time when the Tri-State was built on clay. But the age of American-made dinnerware is over.

Plate 113. This postcard can be purchased at most stores in Chester. I bought mine next door to the building that housed the gas station pictured in Chapter 3.

Plate 114. The Ohio Historical Society's Museum of Ceramics occupies the former post office in East Liverpool. It features an informative slide show about "Crockery City" and beautiful displays of ware from many potteries. Downstairs the museum has re-created several scenes from early plants, including a jigger and ware boy and the decorating room.

Plate 115. Ohio Historical Society Museum of Ceramics.

Plate 115. Ohio Historical Society Museum of Ceramics.

Pottery is in many ways the most human of arts. To create something useful as well as beautiful is civilization at its best. How sad that we in America have, for all practical purposes, lost this art! Our tables are set with plastics that contribute to our era's ecological disasters or with the products of other countries. The creativity, craftsmanship, pride, and workmanship of our American potters has been sacrificed for political and economic advantage.

The fingerprints of early American potters can be seen in the yellow ware and Rockingham ware in the Ohio Museum of Ceramics. These are not the perfect products of a machine nor the flawless jewels of the wealthy. Human hands created the plates and bowls that line my shelves, and they were created for everyday people like me. I imagine the other women who served dinner on my dishes and then washed them. I imagine my father-in-law dipping the cup that I hold. I look for his fingerprints in the glaze.

—Chapter Ten—
Leaving No Plate Unturned

PART I: MARKS AND BACKSTAMPS

When my husband-to-be turned over that first saucer, I had no idea that I would spend half my life studying the underside of dinnerware. When I first began looking, ignorant but enthusiastic, I was delighted to see the familiar backstamp of a bow and arrow or the Harker cartouche (a scroll or shield) on the bottom of a plate. I always felt as if I had struck pay dirt or, rather, pay clay!

But the more I found, the more confused I became. There were too many marks or backstamps (I make no apology for using that word. It is simple and descriptive, a boon to the amateur collector.) Some of the pieces had no marks, and sometimes two plates would be exactly alike but have different marks. And what did the marks mean? Besides identifying this plate as having been made by Harker Pottery, did the mark name the pattern, the shape, or what?

Marks are the first piece of technical information most collectors learn about, but they are not necessarily a good means of identification. Let me explain. Marks are convenient for the retailer because they identify a particular manufacturer, decoration, shape, or line. Customers look for names; they want to know what the decoration or shape or color is called so that they can order by name. Thus, it is advantageous to the retailer to have these names on the back. Retailers also like exclusive rights to a line to reduce competition. Harker was glad to oblige; they sold ware under several "exclusive" labels and used decoration names, shape names, and color names as backstamps. Unfortunately, they were not always consistent.

Marks can be stamped, as most of Harker's were. If the mark is monochrome — in black and white, one color, or gold — it is probably a stamp. These stamps were put on by hand by workers who occasionally made a mistake. Sometimes they missed a piece. Sometimes they stamped a piece twice, once in a while with two different stamps. Usually, a particular stamp was specified, but if the wrong one was used, no one complained except, perhaps, the retailer.

Even more often, the decorating department, who applied the marks as well as the decals and lining, was instructed not to apply a mark! The log that Valma Baxter kept of the department for 1935 notes that decal #7231 -- Amy I -- was not to be stamped as of Dec. 22, 1936. The decal that I call Nasturtium and that Harker called #7279 or #7161 is clearly marked "no stamp" in the log. I had won-dered why I never found a stamp on that line.

Other marks are decals. A mark that uses several colors, as on some of the HotOven ware, is a decal. HotOven and Bakerite labels were put on ware that could stand the heat of an oven. The piece might be a casserole or a plate; the shape or decoration of the ware didn't matter, only that it was heat-proof. Therefore, HotOven and Bakerite marks can be found on a variety of items.

Some marks are part of the mold itself and are impressed into the clay, leaving a mark below the surface, or embossed, leaving a mark raised above the surface of the body. The very earliest marks Harker used as part of Harker, Taylor and Company and Etruria Pottery were impressed. On the Stone China of the 1960's, "Harkerware" is impressed into each piece. Some ware that was destined to be exported was impressed or embossed with simply "Ironstone USA."

An incised mark is made after the clay is taken from the mold. Russel Wright's White Clover and his clocks have his signature incised into most pieces of the line.

So what does the mark tell us? Both a great deal and very little.

First of all, we cannot expect every piece to be marked. I don't usually buy unmarked ware. For example, I am very wary of the big Virginia lug utility plates and the Round Gadroon and Virginia Gadroon plates; Harker sold too many to jobbers. On the other hand, Harker cups, sugar and creamer sets, serving forks and spoons, cake and pie lifters, salt and pepper shakers, and rolling pins were almost never marked because they were too small or because there was no inconspicuous place to put the mark.

The mark may tell us how the ware can be safely used. HotOven and Bakerite were made to withstand the heat of the oven. The mark may also include the words "Dishwasher Safe." (And well they may be, but I am too cautious — to my husband's financial delight — to trust my precious dinnerware to the heat and rigors of a dishwasher!)

The patent mark on Cameoware tells us that the process was owned by Harker. "Made in U.S.A." was used for both legal and promotional reasons, especially on ware made for export. "Good Housekeeping Seal of Approval" was prestigious. Some information on marks is not even totally true. For example, Harker used "East Liverpool, Ohio" on stamps even after the plant moved to Chester, West Virginia.

As a further example, "Pate-Sur-Pate" on Harker means

nothing. The original pate-sur-pate technique developed in France is too time-consuming to be commercially profitable, and the use of the term means no more than a royal coach on a label means that Queen Elizabeth II endorses the product. Pate-sur-Pate was merely an elegant title.

Marks are not even a particularly good means of dating ware. A mark could have been used on ware years after the stamp originated. Pictured earlier in this book were three pieces of the Republic line; two were marked with Harker's embellished arrow and one with the old George S. Harker crossed flags. A period of ten years or more could have separated their production.

I have included all the Harker marks that I have found in rough chronological order, and thanks to many authors who preceded me, the collection of marks is fairly comprehensive, but it probably is not complete or totally accurate. I discovered two marks myself and was shown three by William Gates too late for inclusion. No one has collected all the marks that Harker used in more than 125 years of production, and not all can be documented. I tried whenever possible to limit the dating to years that could be doc-

umented, but the dates in this book and in other books of marks are approximate because accurate records were not kept or have been lost. Books of marks are helpful, but not fired in porcelain.

One Harker mark that is listed in many reputable books is not even a backstamp! I have seen a half-dozen representations of what I call the Embellished Arrow backstamp with the arrow pointing down, but I have never seen an actual piece with such a mark; all the ware have marks with the arrow pointing up. I have not, of course, seen all the Harker ever produced, but it did seem strange that I had never come across a documented mark, a piece with that mark on it, in any book or museum. Then I read the work of William C. Gates, Jr. and Dana E. Ormerod, *The East Liverpool, Ohio, Pottery District: Identification of Manufacturers and Marks.* Gates and Ormerod point out that the arrow pointing down is a logo used on stationery, not on pottery. Since then I have found many letterheads with the arrow down, but no backstamps. Until someone shows me a piece with the arrow down, I believe Gates and Ormerod.

Fig. 36A.

Fig. 36B.

Fig. 36C.

Fig. 38. This documented mark (ca. 1890-1930) was drawn from original ware.

Fig. 36A. Ramsay, Spargo, and others have used variants of this version. **Fig. 36B**. This version with the scrolls above the bow string appears in Thorn's book. **Fig. 36C**. Barber, the foremost early authority on marks, used this hand-drawn version of an authentic documented mark.

Fig. 37. This logo from the letterhead of original Harker correspondence (see typewritten date at right) shows the mark arrow down and labeled "Trade Mark," but I believe that the arrow was inverted for design reasons.

PART II: DECORATIONS

Just as collectors cannot rely solely upon backstamps for identification, neither can they trust the patterns of decorations. Except for the intaglio or engobe process, Harker had few exclusive decorations. The pottery was producing everyday dinnerware, and cost was a big factor. The decals were usually standard designs chosen from manufacturers' stocks. In some cases, Harker bought decals that were also used by a half-dozen other potteries. The decoration that Harker called Godey (although it does not look like a Godey illustration) and the Currier & Ives prints were and still are used on every conceivable ceramic product by hundreds of manufacturers. The lovely Pastel Tulip and varieties of Petit Point were used by several other potteries as well as Harker.

I have found the Amy decal, which I thought was a Harker exclusive, on a plate with an embossed floral rim like no Harker product I have ever seen. It has no backstamp, so I don't know if it is a case of another pottery using Amy or of Harker using a shape that I have never seen. And I am currently trying to solve the mystery of a small round Gadroon dessert plate with the Lovelace decal that is marked "Ambrosia China" in block letters. Was this another Harker backstamp? Or did another pottery make the plate on a Harker blank?

All of this means that we collectors can't really depend upon the pattern of decoration on the ware. If we pick up a plate with no backstamp and a decal used by several potteries, how can we tell who actually manufactured it? Lois Lehner gives the answer in each of her books in italics or underlined or in all capitals, and the smart collector carries the message always: "SHAPE IS THE KEY TO IDENTIFYING DINNERWARE." The problem is a little like putting together a jigsaw puzzle; by learning to recognize the shapes or molds that Harker -- or any other pottery -- used, we can be relatively sure of our purchases.

PART III: SHAPES

Each pottery used its own molds, but just like clothing designers, dinnerware manufacturers copied each other's successful lines and abandoned unsuccessful ones. And just as a designer may stretch a fashion line by making old favorites in new fabrics, potteries resurrected favorite molds regularly and decorated them in new patterns.

The only way to recognize the shapes of a particular pottery is to pick up and inspect a great many examples. It's like the old story about finding a prince by kissing a lot of frogs, except you don't have to kiss the pottery. Handle it, study it, compare it. Study the photos in this book and others. Soon you will be able to walk into an antique store or flea market and spot the Harker pieces immediately. My husband claims that I can smell them, but it is actually the same visual sense that makes me a good jigsaw puzzle solver: I recognize the shape of the pieces.

PART IV: CARING FOR AND FEEDING YOUR HARKER COLLECTION

Feeding your collection is easy; your problem will be curbing your appetite. In more than 125 years of production, Harker made almost everything, and because the prices are still relatively low, you can actually buy too much. Unless you learn to concentrate on one area, you can end up storing your collection in boxes in the basement. I swore I would never do that, but in the process of writing this book, because I was eager to show as many patterns, shapes, and marks as possible, I bought pieces that I had no intention of keeping. When this book is in print, those parts of my collection will be sold off.

Specialization is the key to a good collection. If you are mad about flowers, collect flower patterns. Like miniatures? Look for unusual sugar and creamer or shaker sets. Are you a master chef? Look for the kitchenware like rolling pins, scoops, and so on. I want to specialize in the intaglio patterns and in older lines made from 1890 to 1930 and learn all I can about them.

Also I want to replace objects that are not in mint condition with better examples. What does "mint condition" mean? To some, it means "in the original sales condition." I know someone who has pieces of dinnerware in the original boxes with the original seals, but most of us will settle for something less. Mint condition items should have no flaws: no scratches, chips, cracks (and a "hairline" is still a crack), or repairs. Decorations, including hand-painting and metal trim, should be complete, unfaded, and not discolored.

Crazing, the fine webbed lines on the surface, is common for less expensive ware like Harker's, but it is a matter of degree. So is the problem of uneven glazing and "pin marks," tiny pits left by the pins that held the pieces apart as they were fired. The collector must be willing to compromise on minor flaws. I consider them part of the charm and the history of the products, but I am careful to avoid repairs, alterations in the original glaze, and "marriages," the use of a lid that does not match the original (A missing lid usually halves the so-called "book price.")

Once an object is yours, care for it. Start by getting it home literally in one piece. If you can, wrap it yourself in your own materials. Carry tape, wrapping paper, and bags with you. Tape lids on securely. Wrap the pieces individually in newspaper or tissue (Some dealers recommend using disposable diapers), but don't leave china wrapped in newsprint too long because the ink can discolor it. Don't stack cups inside one another because the handles can crack and friction can damage decorations. Use your own carrying bag, too. Ever since I lost a whole day's harvest when the handles on the dealer's "recycled" bag broke, I now carry a heavy canvas tote bag.

On the way home, secure your purchases carefully. A heavy cardboard box wedged in the back seat where it cannot move or be crushed will do the job. When Don and I travel, one cupboard in the trailer is devoted to storing my keepsakes. I wrap them carefully and tuck towels or sheets around them. We carry bubble wrap to protect them, and I have considered buying divided boxes made for storing Christmas ornaments. One friend suggested zippered dinnerware cases, but I am too frugal. I made my own — simple bags from scraps of quilted fabric. We also could ship them home by using wrapping and shipping services that are available nationwide.

We use our dishes. They decorate our home and we eat every meal from them. Plates and other display pieces hang in every room in the house, including the bathrooms, but we do use some caution. We prefer plastic-coated hangers to prevent chips and wear on the plate edges, and we display other items on yards of wide shelves with dowels to hold the items in place.

If a piece is badly crazed and dirt has accumulated in the crazing, I have used bleach successfully to soak the damage away. I put the item in a plastic bucket that I reserve for this purpose and cover the item with Clorox. Some stains disappear immediately; others take several days or even weeks. I once left a badly stained jug in the bucket while we went on a three-week vacation, and the jug survived beautifully. However, some stains, especially baked-in grease, do not ever completely disappear.

Sometimes a powdery residue forms on the object, but this washes off. If the odor of chlorine lingers, a soaking in washing soda or vinegar takes care of the problem. I have had no success removing stains with damp salt or borax, and I don't want to risk using industrial-strength peroxide.

I wash my dishes promptly and carefully in hot, not scalding, water immediately after use to avoid acid and alkali stains and also to avoid the use of abrasives. I do not trust a dishwasher because it can damage gold and platinum trims as well as fade decorations. A plastic dishpan, rubber sink mats, and a rubber collar on the faucet spout prevent accidental chips and breakage. Between stored flatware, I use padded liners made of old scraps of quilted fabric cut into circles and edge-stitched. I also try to rotate the dishes so that all get equal wear.

The HotOven, Bakerite, and Modern Age can be used in the oven, but I rarely do so. I prefer to use them merely as serving pieces after the food has been heated in other, less-valuable bowls. I have used some in the microwave, but after a shower of sparks, I learned not to put gold- or platinum-trim in the microwave.

Keep careful records of your collection for insurance purposes, if for no other reason. Contact your insurance agent about protecting your dishes from theft and fire, if not breakage. I use duplicate computer records, but written file cards will work as well if kept up to date. Of course, the organization system that you use is up to you, but be sure to record the shape name and the backstamp as well as the item's name and pattern. Your insurance agent will want the price that you paid recorded. It also helps to add notes on condition and unusual features. Photographs or video tapes can also be used as documentation.

Most of all, enjoy your collection. Shop for new pieces in every flea market and antique shop you see. Read about other collections and other histories. Rearrange your shelves to show off new acquisitions. Find other collectors who will understand when you gloat over your newest bargain or unique treasure.

I hope that you found this book useful, readable, and entertaining. I hope to hear from collectors and to learn that new dinnerware fanciers have joined me in collecting Harker Pottery, USA.

Although Harker was not the first or the last American pottery to succumb to economic disaster, their closing was significant: the death of the oldest continually run family-owned pottery in the United States. From 1840 to 1969 the Harker and Boyce families lived the American Dream; they made a small but concrete contribution to American enterprise as they helped two small American towns to flourish. Harker Pottery served as a seedbed for the ceramics industry of the Ohio Valley and trained many of the founders of other American potteries. The Harker craftspeople and artisans proudly created dinnerware and cookware that reflected the history of changing American tastes. The factory is gone; the founders sleep in a quiet cemetery high above the river; the potters are dispersed to other factories, retired, or deceased. But when a collector holds a plate with the Harker mark on the back, he holds a piece of all of them and a piece of America in his hand.

Glossary

AU GRATIN CASSEROLE AND TRAY
A small covered casserole (about three cups) set on a 7" plate.

BAKER
An open oval vegetable dish or a "pie baker," a 9" or 10" pie pan.

BASIN
The large bowl that was part of a wash set.

BEEHIVE KILN
The earliest kilns in the East Liverpool area were shaped like a bottle or beehive with a stack rising above it.

BLANK
An undecorated, often unfired basic shape.

BODY
The basic clay form of a ceramic item.

BRUSH VASE
A small vase used to hold toothbrushes. Part of a wash set.

CABINET
A slop jar with a wire bail or handle. An uncovered slop jar with no handle was a CUSPIDORE.

CASSEROLE
Although to housewives this refers to an oven-safe covered bowl of any shape, to potters it was a round covered vegetable dish. An oval covered dish was called simply a covered dish.

CERAMICS
All products made from clay. Because of the similarities in the manufacturing processes, glass and enameled products not made of clay are frequently included.

CHEESE TRAY
An 11" round plate, usually Zephyr, sold with a small (about 1 cup) covered casserole called a cheese box.

CHINA
Once meant only porcelain. Most of us use it today to mean whatever we eat meals from, be it porcelain, paper. or plastic.

CHOP PLATE
A large (10" or more) plate usually with lugs (handles) and often shallowly depressed to hold meat juices.

COOKING WARE
Any oven-safe ware.

COUPE
(Pronounced "koop.") Means that the body of the plate, bowl, or dish is curved upward at the edge and lacks a flat rim.

CRAZE
Tiny cracks in the glaze caused by the difference in contracting of the body and glaze.

DECAL or DECALCOMANIA
A special design-bearing sheet used in decorating. The sheet is first applied with varnish or another medium to the ware. The paper backing is then removed by soaking in water, resulting in the transfer of the colored pattern to the ware. Subsequent firing makes it permanent. Decals may be applied over glazes or under them. A decal over the glaze is brighter in color, but vulnerable to damage.

DINNERWARE
Clay products used for consumption of food.

DIPPING
The process by which the body is dipped in or sprayed with engobe or glaze prior to firing. Before machines were used, dippers used metal braces on their fingers to hold the

ware and twirl it to distribute the color evenly.

DISH

Often merely a shallow bowl or shallowly depressed plate. Also an oval meat dish or platter.

EARTHENWARE

White or light-colored clayware relatively inexpensive to produce because it is made of clay fired at comparatively low temperatures. Heavier and more porous than porcelain and without porcelain's strength, translucence, and resonance, it is well-suited to everyday use.

EMBOSSED

Having a design raised above the surface as opposed to one carved into the surface. See INTAGLIO.

ENGOBE

Liquid clay. In the intaglio process, engobe is sprayed over bisque and then cut away to reveal the white layer below.

EWER

A large water pitcher, part of a wash set. A smaller hot-water pitcher was called a MOUTH EWER.

FLATWARE

Plates, platters, or saucers of any size. Potters did not use the same terminology that housewives do for such items; they made no distinction between a dinner, luncheon, salad, or bread and butter plate. They were simply referred to by size: 9" plate, 7" plate, 6" plate and 5" plate.

FOOTED BOWL

A bowl set on a narrowed raised base, or "foot."

FRUIT

A small (5" diameter) dessert dish.

GADROON

A molded dinnerware decoration which resembles braided rope.

GLAZE

A glassy layer covering a ceramic body that is fired until the coating becomes hard and permanent. There are as many kinds of glaze as there are kinds of glass.

GRANITE WARE

Smooth, heavy white earthenware that resembles English ironstone. Used primarily for commercial purposes in hotels and restaurants.

HOLLOW WARE

Cups, bowls, pitchers, etc. Any body that is hollow.

INTAGLIO

A design carved into a flat surface. Harker's intaglio involved using a reverse stencil or stencil to blast away the engobe surface to reveal the white body beneath. The body was then glazed.

IRIDESCENCE

A glaze that produces a rainbow effect like mother-of-pearl on the surface. It is not the same as luster; lusterware is made with a metallic base, often copper.

IRONSTONE

An historic term for durable English stoneware, similar to porcelain except that the body is not translucent and is off-white, almost gray. In more recent times, the term has been used for any heavy white ware. In the United States, it is sometimes called opaque porcelain or semi-porcelain.

JIGGER

A craftsman who forms flatware on a jig, a mold. A jigger needs speed, experience, good judgment, and capable assistants.

JUG

The potter's name for a pitcher of any size.

KILN

Pronounced "kill" by potters, an oven in which clay is "fired" or baked to its proper degree of hardness.

LINING

A decoration of lines, one or many, applied by hand or machine.

LUG

Small tab handles on a piece of flatware or on bowls.

LUSTER

A metallic coating, usually copper, on ceramics.

MARRIAGES

A mating of two different patterns, shapes, or lines of pottery. The marriage pieces may be from totally different sources.

MOLD

A form used for shaping hollow ware pieces.

NAPPY
The potter's name for a an open round vegetable dish.

OVENWARE
Clayware that is ovensafe. Cookware that can be also used for table service.

OVERGLAZE DECORATION
Applied after firing and glazing, these are brighter in color, but vulnerable to damage.

PASTE
The mixture of clay and other products from which dinnerware is made. The differences between soft paste and hard paste are the additives.

PATE SUR PATE
Ornamentation created by painting layers of paste one upon another and then carving away to form a design.

PIN MARKS
Small pits in the bottom of finished ware left by the pins, clay sticks that separate layers of ware in the kilns.

PLAIN ROUND or OVAL
Flatware with raised flat rim.

PORCELAIN
A hard, translucent clayware that is generally used interchangeably with the word *china*. Made of kaolin, feldspars, china stone, and flint, porcelain is delicate, thin, dense and vitrified (nonporous).

POTTERY
Technically, anything made by a potter. Usually the term is used for products made of clay only without additives and of coarse, porous quality.

RIBBED COLLAR
Exactly as the name implies, a design of vertical lines like ribbing set near neck or waist of the body.

ROCKINGHAM
Refers to products made of buff clay and glazed in dark brown, frequently mottled. Bennington is a pottery that produced Rockingham ware in New England.

SAGGERS
Ceramic containers in which clay bodies, held in place by clay pins, are stacked in order to be fired in the kiln. The saggers are reused, but the pins are broken and discarded.

SAUCE BOAT
What you and I call a gravy boat.

SEMI-PORCELAIN
An American name for hard white body developed in the 1880's and considered the same kind of ware as English ironstone. It was not translucent but was semi-vitrified. Often called semi-porcelain, it was halfway between porcelain and earthenware. Durable, not easily broken, but not translucent.

SHOULDER
The raised rim of a traditionally shaped plate.

SLIP
Clay mixed with water to a creamy consistency.

SLIP COATING
A layer of slip applied to clayware body for a decorative effect. Engobe.

SPITTOON
A cuspidor.

STONEWARE or STONE CHINA
A non-porous ceramic body made of unprocessed clay or of clay and additives like silica or flint. Fired at high temperatures, it is durable, resists chipping, and rings true, but lacks porcelain's whiteness.

TABLEWARE
Includes both dinnerware and serving pieces.

THIRDS
Ware that could not meet standards set by the individual pottery. Usually SECONDS were flawed but decorated and stamped to be sold through the pottery's outlet store. THIRDS were not stamped, but were decorated with leftover decals and sold in large lots to retailers.

TOILETWARE
Clay products used for sanitary or personal hygiene.

VIRGINIA
A squared-off plate shape with scalloped corners. Made in both plain edge and Gadroon. The utility plate has lugs.

WHITE GRANITE
Another name for semi-porcelain. Heavy-duty white ware used for hotel china and sanitary ware.

WHITE WARE

A generic name for ceramics made with clay that is white or almost white. White earthenware was most common in the East Liverpool area, and porcelain not common at all.

TEXTURE GLAZE

Using colored glaze that runs, drips, bubbles, or is deliberately disturbed to add decoration.

TOBY JUG or MUG

A pitcher or cup that resembles a man. It may represent all or just a portion of his figure.

TRANSFER PRINTING

An early process of decoration in which a monochrome design was transferred to the ware and then usually hand-colored.

TRANSLUCENCE

The degree to which light can be seen through the finished piece. Fine porcelain allows much light through, heavier clays less.

TUNNEL KILN

A large, long kiln shaped like a tunnel through which saggers of ware move on tracks.

UNDERGLAZE DECORATION

Applied before the ware receives its final clear glaze, these decorations have less intense color, but are more enduring.

UTILITY PLATE

A large, multipurpose serving plate. For Harker, the 12" lugged Virginia usually was used.

VITREOUS/VITRIFIED

Non-porous, therefore it resists stains.

YELLOW WARE

The cheapest plainest form of pottery in America made of buff-burning clay. Usually undecorated, it sometimes had colored bands or sponge decoration added.

—Selected Sources—

Advertisements. *China & Glass Trade Directory.* Pittsburgh: China, Glass and Lamps, 1927-39.

Advertisement. *China, Glass and Lamps.* December 1936:7.

Baker, Tim. "Community's Pride Is Still Brewing." *The Intelligencer* (Wheeling,WV) 16 March 1991: 1-2.

Barber, Edwin Atlee. *The Pottery and Porcelain of the United States and Marks of American Potters.* Combined edition. New York: Feingold & Lewis, 1976. Preface by Diana and J.G. Stradling.

Baxter, Valma. Personal Interviews. 1992.

Boger, Louise Ade. *The Dictionary of World Pottery and Porcelain.* New York: Scribner's, 1971.

Boyce, David G. Speech at Harker Christmas Party as transcribed by Grace Mahon. 23 December 1960.

Boyce, Robert E. Harker Employee Bulletin. Ms. 25 April 1956.

Cameron, Elizabeth. *Encyclopedia of Pottery & Porcelain: 1800-1960.* New York: Facts on File, 1986.

Cashdollar, Roy C. *A History of Chester: The Gateway to the West.* Wheeling,WV: Boyd Press, N.D.

"Ceramic History: Centenary Anniversary of Harker Pottery Company." Excerpts from article by Lucille T. Cox, *East Liverpool Review* 5 Jan. 1940.

Cox, Lucille T. "Forgotten Town of Chester? There Was One." *East Liverpool Review* n.d., n. pag.

--------------. "Harker 'Won and Lost' on Shipment of Clay." *East Liverpool Review* 25 Nov. 1938: n. pag.

--------------. "What's in a Name? Etruria Pleased Potters." *East Liverpool Review* 20 Sept. 1940: n. pag.

Cunningham, Jo. *The Collector's Encyclopedia of American Dinnerware.* Paducah, KY: Collector Books, 1982.

De Forest, Michael. *Antiquing from A to Z : Buying & Selling Antiques, Collectibles & Other Old Things.* New York: Simon and Schuster, 1975.

Derwich, Jenny B., and Dr. Mary Latos. *Dictionary Guide to United States Pottery & Porcelain: 19th and 20th Century.* Franklin, MI: Jenstan, 1984.

"Domestic Pottery Industry Approaching 100th Brithday." *Pottery, Glass & Brass Salesman* March 1939: 8-9+.

"The Etruria Pottery." *East Liverpool Times* 25 March 1876: n. pag.

Gates, William C. Jr. *The City of Hills & Kilns: Life and Work in East Liverpool, Ohio.* East Liverpool: East Liverpool Historical Society, 1984.

Gates, William C., Jr., and Dana E. Ormerod. *The East Liverpool, Ohio, Pottery District: Identification of Manufacturers and Marks.* Ann Arbor: The Society for Historical Archaeology, 1982.

Gilchrist, Brenda, ed. *The Smithsonian Illustrated Library of Antiques: Pottery.* Compiled for the Cooper-Hewitt Museum, the Smithsonian Institution's National Museum of Design. Washington, DC, 1981.

Heaivilin, Annise Doring. *Grandma's Tea Leaf Ironstone.* Des Moines: Wallace-Homestead, 1981.

Johnson, Bruce E. "Antiques Across America." *Country Living* Sept. 1990:52+.

Ketchum, William C.,Jr. *The Pottery & Porcelain Collector's Handbook: A Guide to Early American Ceramics from Maine to California.* New York: Funk & Wagnalls, 1971.

Lehner, Lois. *Lehner's Encyclopedia of U.S. Marks on Pottery, Porcelain, & Clay.* Paducah, KY: Collector Books, 1988.

------------. *Ohio Pottery and Glass: Marks and Manufacturers.* DesMoines: Wallace-Homestead, 1978.

Love, Madeline. "Showroom by Showroom." *China, Glass and Lamps* Feb. 1937:16.

Oldest Pottery in America Marks Its 125th Anniversary." *China, Glass and Tablewares* Jan. 1965:24-5.

Pinney, Paul. Personal Interviews. 1991-1992.

Press Release. Harker China Company. Ms. n.d.

Ramsay, John. *American Potters and Pottery.* New York: Tudor Publishing, 1947.

Spargo, John. *Early American Pottery and China.* New York: Century, 1926.

Svec, J.J., ed. *Pottery Production Processes.* (Prepared as series of articles in *Ceramic Industry*) Chicago: Industrial Publications, 1946.

Stiles, Helen E. *Pottery in the United States.* New York: Dutton, 1941.

Thorn, C. Jordan. *Handbook of Old Pottery and Porcelain Marks.* New York: Tudor, 1947.

Trimble, Alberta C. *Modern Porcelain: Today's Treasures Tomorrow's Traditions.* New York: Bonanza Books, 1968.

Value Guide
Listing of Patterns, Colors, and Shapes

The first thing we collectors want to know about a piece is its name. We want to be confident in discussing the piece with other collectors and matching pieces by name. Unfortunately, this is not always possible.

Potteries did not bother to name most of their decorations. They used catalog numbers if necessary. When they did name a decoration in catalogs or brochures, they were inconsistent at best. One decorative pattern might have had a dozen different names depending on the whim of the retailer, the pottery, or the workers. Names of decals were changed frequently as the body shape changed.

Whenever possible, I have tried to use the name that Harker used if I could document it through advertisements, catalogs, order forms, and memos. If I could not do so, the next best solution was to use the name commonly used by other researchers. And when that failed, I made up a name based on the appearance of the decoration or my feelings about it. Some of the older patterns I have named after people I love. As I discover the names Harker actually used, I shall revise my catalog, but by then I shall probably find new nameless patterns that I can christen.

Then we have the problem of names garnered from research that have no illustration or even description. I have no idea what "Amethyst," "Velvet," and "Primrose" look like. Amethyst and Velvet may not even be patterns, but colors or shapes. These names have appeared in listings in books or in sales literature from Harker. Sometimes we find an "orphan," a name or decoration that seems to have been the sole survivor of a line. These were often samples that were used in the big annual trade shows in January and July. If no interest was shown in the line, production ceased or was never begun.

Next, we collectors want to know when the piece was made. We can make only an educated guess based on a number of clues. I have given the earliest documented date I could find for the decorations, the glazes, the shapes and marks in this appendix, but most are only approximations. Even a date on a Harker sales memo could be for ware that was made years before.

Of course, we also want some guidance in what is a fair price. We want to know if we are paying too much or being paid too little. This really opens a philosophic and economic can of worms.

Technically, little of Harker can even be classified as antique. If one accepts the usual rule of 100 years, then only the ware made before 1890 — yellow ware and Rockingham — is really antique.

Harker dinnerware is a collectible, that undefined and undefinable area that covers anything that any two people — one to sell and one to buy — collect!

The value of a collectible, like beauty, is in the eye of the beholder. I once offended a flea-market vendor by remarking to my husband within the vendor's hearing that a certain piece of Harker "wasn't worth it." The vendor began to berate me loudly, and I replied equally rudely. In retrospect, we were both right. The saucer was worth to him what he asked ... but not to me.

And once when a lady in an antique shop asked me — the so-called "expert" — what a piece of ware was worth, I hedged and ended by really saying nothing worthwhile. She was disappointed and felt that I had let her down. I had, but I could not get across to her that her pretty little dish had no real value except what it was worth to her and to a buyer. They must reach a compromise between them on a fair price. Neither I nor anyone else could put an absolute value on what was essentially valueless.

After all, pottery has little intrinsic value. Ceramics — even the finest porcelain — is ephemeral because it is too easily broken. Once damaged, the fragments cannot be turned into anything else of value. Even the gold and platinum trim cannot be recovered. There is really little difference between a broken Harker pottery cup and a broken Ming vase, except that a museum may be willing to pay for the shards of the Ming.

Some authorities divide dinnerware and other items as "collectible" and "not collectible." I like to make a distinction between collectible with an "i" and collectable with an "a." "Collectible" refers to anything that people collect; "collectable" refers to its market value. Anything then is collectible, but not everything is collectable; that is, salable at the price the seller wants.

I have no problem either with spending more than "book value" on a piece that I like or with passing up a "bargain" if it is not something that I like. It is my collection. If some day an heir makes a few dollars on my collection, fine, but I am not cashing in my annuities to enhance some theoretical value.

Knowing the current marketplace value of an object merely gives guidelines as to what one must be prepared to pay. The guidelines do not, however, reflect what a collector can expect for an item; dealers have to make a profit, so they are not going to pay a collector "book price" for an item.

The values in this book bear no relation to the absolute

value of dinnerware. These are honest, realistic guidelines to what dealers are asking and, presumably, collectors are paying. All items pictured in this book are priced according to, first of all, what they actually cost me. If they were gifts or if the pieces are not first-class condition, I used the current prices in antique and collectible stores and flea markets through the Ohio Valley and the Northeast for mint condition pieces. For items from the Ohio Museum of Ceramics, I tried to find articles of comparable design and quality in antique shops.

Because there is so much Harker ware available and even though it has not become widely recognized, collectors will find a wide range of prices. So, I have given a low, which is usually the flea market or garage sale price, and a high, usually the price of antique stores. If the reader finds some of the values unreasonably high or low, probably I did too, but these are real prices. If I have been unable to find another example or a comparable item, I have used the only price I found.

All the pieces in this book are listed except those for which I can give no price because they are museum-quality or one-of-a-kind items. Starred items are ones that I have passed by, but consider interesting, such as the Chesterton egg cup in Chocolate Brown. I didn't buy it, and I have never seen another one. NFS equals Not For Sale, no value was determined.

I am ignoring backstamps altogether in my value guides for good reasons that I outlined earlier. Except for advertising items, souvenirs, and other specialties, items are listed by pattern because that is the most easily recognized. In cases where the pattern is unknown, but the shape is named, I have listed the piece by that. I have also included color and glaze names that I could document.

Acorn

Unknown intaglio pattern said to be on Sears' Harmony House mark.

Advertising

[NOTE: Prices vary widely based not only upon condition, but also on the subject, the advertiser, the item, and so on.]

American Flag 8" plain round plate	$3.00-30.00
Boy and Dog plate	$3.00-30.00
Bunny in the Snow 9" coupe plate	$3.00-30.00
Campbell Kid dish	$10.00-22.00
East Liverpool C.of C. plates	$3.00-30.00
Fox in the Snow	$3.00-30.00
Harker Pottery ashtray	$2.00-6.00
Grapefruit decal dish	$3.00-30.00
Iridescent rim landscape plate	$3.00-30.00
Japanese decal jug (premium)	$10.00-25.00
Kelvinator leftover keeper	$8.00-30.00
Miner's & Mechanics cylindrical ashtray	$3.00-8.00
Silver Dollar ashtray 6" Gadroon	$2.00-6.00
*Spencer Plan trivet	$22.00-45.00
Strawberry berry bowl	$3.00-30.00

"Surprised"- Deer at Stream	$3.00-30.00
"Thoroughbreds" - Sheep in pasture	$3.00-30.00
Waterford Park ashtray	$2.00-6.00
Webber trivet	$245.00

Aladdin shape
(ca. 1952) See also Slender Leaf.

Teal rose dinner plate	$2.00-10.00
Celadon platinum creamer	$2.00-5.00
Gravy pitcher with teal rose	$4.00-14.00
*Gray teapot, no backstamp	$22.00
*Ivy on teal teapot, cream & sugar, salt & pepper	$50.00

Alpine
(ca. 1957) Harker name for intaglio pattern of white spruce spray with turquoise accent on pink-cocoa.

6" plate	$1.00-5.00

Amber
Listed in 1967 ad as a color of stoneware.

Ambrosia
(ca.1960) Harker name for unknown decal. See Lovelace.

Amethyst
Unknown pattern.

Amy
(ca. 1935) Actually two decals of pastel flowers in peach and white with HotOven and Red Arrow marks. Amy I is of orange, red, and white poppies with forget-me-nots, applied to Puritan ware. Amy II has an orange poppy and a white rose with forget-me-nots. See also White Rose.

6" embossed edge plate	$1.00-5.00
Dinner plate	$2.00-10.00
Casserole	$7.00-36.00
Spoon and lifter set	$12.00-42.00
*Teapot	$17.00
*Hi-Rise jug	$22.00

Anemone
My name for decal of bright flowers with black accents.

12" Virginia utility plate	$8.00-40.00
Cake/pie lifter	$5.00-20.00
Two-piece cylindrical stackable	$5.00-10.00
Spoon	$5.00-20.00

Antique Auto
(ca.1960) Harker name for decals used by other potteries as well. Also called Old-Fashioned Autos.

Jumbo cup and saucer	$8.00-22.00
8" Virginia Gadroon plate	$2.00-10.00

Dinner plate $2.00-10.00
4-5" coupe ashtray $1.00-3.00
5-6" round Gadroon ashtray............................$2.00-6.00

Apples & Nuts
My name for old (pre-1930) decal.

Dinner plate $2.00-10.00

Arches
(from 1890) Also called Ropes and Arches. Used primarily on bowls, it was a trim of rope above arched mold.

Argonaut
(ca.1900) Toilet set with rounded body and ribbed collar.

Asters
My name for decal of small aster-like flowers.

Miniature Regal jug.................................$5.00-25.00

Auntie Q.
My name for decal of a yellow rose and other flowers.

Square casserole $12.00

Autumn Leaf
Jewel Tea's line of ware with brown and orange leaf pattern. Reportedly made under Columbia mark.

Avocado
Listed by Lehner as a color of the Chesterton and Concord series.

Bamboo
(ca.1955) Harker name for intaglio pattern of bamboo on pink-cocoa.

*Lunch plate $8.00

Basket
Cunningham's name for decal of a single basket of flowers.

Basket of Flowers
My name for various decals of flowers in a basket.

Vegetable bowl $2.00-15.00
*Skyscraper range set (drip jar/shakers)......................$17.00
Columbia stamp hexagonal ashtray/trivet............$4.00-10.00

Becky
Cunningham's name for decal of blue and orange flowers.

Bedford
(ca. 1900) Harker called it "square shape" in their catalog. An old complete line of dinnerware.

Bermuda
(ca. 1949) Harker name for decal of blue and gray leaves on Gadroon. Also used (Bermuda Blue) as the name for light blue Chesterton.

Lunch plate $2.00-8.00

Birds and Flowers
Cunningham's name for decal of stylized fringed flowers and blue birds.

*Cup and saucer.....................................$7.00

Black-eyed Susan
(ca.1957) Harker name for intaglio pattern of white daisies with brown centers. Also called Brown-eyed Susan.

Cup $1.00-5.00
6" saucer..$1.00-2.00
6" plate $1.00-5.00
Dinner plate $2.00-10.00
Cake set with 6" plates $5.00-10.00
1-tier tidbit tray $3.00-6.00
*2-tier tidbit tray $24.00
3-tier tidbit tray $5.00-20.00
Plain Yellow cake/pie lifter.......................$5.00-20.00

Blanche
My name for older floral pattern on embossed edge.

Dinner plate $2.00-10.00

Blue and Gold Band
My name for design of wide blue band embellished with gold floral scrolls.

5" fruit dish......................................$1.00-5.00

Blue Basket
My name for old decal of blue basket filled with orange, gold and blue flowers.
Gem cream pitcher.................................$3.00-7.00
Souvenir plate of Versailles Court House.............$3.00-30.00

Blue Berry
(ca. 1935) Also Red Berry. Harker name for decal of stylized stem of black leaves and blue berries with Red Arrow stamp.

Blue Blossoms
Cunningham's name for decal of apple blossoms and blue wisteria.

Blue Doily
(ca. 1935) Also Red Doily. Harker name for unknown decals.

Blue Grapes
My name for older pattern of grapes.

    Pie baker $5.00-25.00

Blue Mist
(ca.1952) Robin's egg blue with tiny flecks used on Stone China.

Blue Rhythm
(ca.1959) Harker name for intaglio in pale blue on Gadroon shape under Sears' Harmony House mark.

    Dinner plate $2.00-10.00

Bottle Green
(ca. 1960) Used on Rockingham Reproductions.

Bouquet
Cunningham's name for a blue and tan flower, leaf, and stem. In 1949, Harker used this name for a design on Gadroon of pastel tulips and roses surrounded by a circle of matching flowers.

    Cup $1.00-5.00

Boyce
Cunningham's name for decal of pink and blue flowers.

    *Regal jug (stained)..$24.00

Bridal Rose
(ca.1935-49) Harker name for a decal of swags of tiny pink roses.

    Dinner plate $2.00-10.00
    Swirl vegetable bowl $2.00-11.00

Brim
Cunningham's name for a provincial border design of blue and rust.

    *Mixing Bowl...$36.00

Cabbage Roses
My name for a collection of old rose patterns.

    Dinner plate, pink roses, green edge line............$3.00-18.00
    Dinner plate, yellow roses, gold rim $3.00-18.00
    *Vegetable dish, yellow roses, signed decal $35.00

    Pittston, PA, souvenir plate with roses.................$3.00-30.00
    Turquoise dresser tray $50.00-100.00

Cable
(ca. 1900) Granite ware line decorated with rope-like handles.

Cactus
My name for Mexican design under Bakerite mark.

    *Zephyr cheese plate $15.00
    12" Virginia utility plate $8.00-40.00
    Pie baker $5.00-25.00
    Rolling pin...$25.00-120.00

Calendar plates

    1907 Christmas plate.......................................$45.00-80.00
    1913 Horses inside horseshoe...........................$15.00-25.00
    1913 Washington's headquarters $15.00-25.00
    1915 Panama Canal plate $15.00-25.00
    *1917 Eagle & Flag...$17.00
    1929 tea tile/calendar $20.00-30.00
    1960 on Heritance shape.................................$1.00-5.00

Calico
(ca.1960) Harker name for decal of birds and flowers on Stone China under the Countrytime USA mark.

Calico Ribbon
(ca. 1935) My name for pattern of red and white check ribbon. Harker decorating department called it Plaid. Also made in brown, yellow, green, and possibly blue.

    Flat cake plate...$5.00-15.00
    Mixing bowl $5.00-40.00

Calico Tulip
Tulip decal in red and blue check on ovenware and dinnerware.

    12" Virginia utility plate $8.00-40.00
    Condiment jar with metal lid $4.00-6.00
    *4 condiment jar set with lids and rack.........................$39.00

Cameo Rose
A misnomer. It usually refers either to the original Dainty Flower intaglio or to the design called White Rose under the Carv-Kraft backstamp. Harker did not use this name for either.

Cameoware
(ca. 1935) The most common line under the Cameo stamp was the design called Dainty Flower. The dinnerware line

included almost every shape Harker made, but the most cookware was on the Zephyr shape. Flatware was made on plain round, Virginia, and Swirl. The Swirl shape was most often referred to as Shellware. Hollow ware was made on Gem, flared, and spherical shapes, and the shaker sets on Skyscraper, Modern Age, and D'Ware. I have seen every shape except Gadroon, and I'll probably find it tomorrow. See also Shellware.

Carla
My name for older pattern in gray and black with yellow dandelions.

12" plain oval platter $5.00-11.00

Carnivale
Stylized pattern of leaves and flowers with black dots.

6" Virginia plate $2.00-5.00
Salad fork server $5.00-20.00
Custard $2.00-10.00
Regal/gargoyle pitcher...$24.00-30.00

Cathy
My name for older pattern of orange and white poppies.

Vegetable bowl $2.00-11.00

Celadon
Chinese gray-green used on Chesterton and intaglio.

Celeste
(ca.1930) Pale blue used on Newport shape. Also called Celestial Blue and used as part of stamp. Later used on Chesterton.

Celeste Primrose
(1960) Harker name for unknown decal on Royal Gadroon.

Charcoal
Used on Chesterton, White Clover, and Stone China intaglio.

Chartreuse
Undocumented. Probably refers to yellow-green shade used on Sun Valley.

Cherry
Cunningham's name for decal of red, yellow, and purple cherries.

Cherry Blossom

Older design of cherries and blossoms.

Dinner plate $2.00-10.00
Dresser tray $5.00-20.00
Giant mixing bowl $10.00-50.00

Cherry Trim
Cunningham's name for decal of gold, red, and purple stylized cherries.

*Sugar bowl in Embassy $10.00

Chesterton (Bermuda Blue)
"Chesterton" is both the name of a line, a shape, and the color silver-gray. "Bermuda Blue" is the name used for the color pale blue on Chesterton and a backstamp.

*13 Pc. coffee set..$10.00
Dinner plate $2.00-10.00
1-tier tidbit tray $3.00-6.00
Gravy boat $4.00-14.00

Chesterton (Chocolate Brown)

*7 pc. odd lot $15.00
*Egg cup $5.00
Cup $1.00-5.00
6" saucer..$1.00-2.00
6" plate $1.00-5.00

Chesterton (Celadon)

Cup $1.00-5.00
6" saucer..$1.00-2.00
Shaker..$1.00-2.00
*Cream and sugar set..$12.00

Chesterton (Charcoal)

*13" platter..$8.00
5" fruit dish..$1.00-5.00

Chesterton (Coral)

*6" plate..$.50

Chesterton (Silver-Gray)
This color is also called Chesterton, and this ware is frequently backstamped Chesterton.

*12 pc gray/pink snack set..$60.00
Gray cup with pink interior $1.00-5.00
Cup..$1.00-5.00
6" saucer..$1.00-2.00
Cup & saucer set..$5.00-10.00
5" fruit dish..$1.00-5.00

6" plate $1.00-5.00
8" Virginia Gadroon plate................................$2.00-10.00
Dinner plate $2.00-10.00
Lugged soup/cereal dish $2.00-5.00
Vegetable bowl $2.00-11.00
Platters $5.00-20.00
Cream and sugar set $5.00-20.00
*Creamer only $5.50
Shaker set $2.00-6.00
Gravy jug $4.00-14.00

Chesterton (Lime)
Frequently backstamped Sun Valley.

*25 pc. odd lot $20.00
6" plate $1.00-5.00

Chesterton (Pink Cocoa)

6" plate $1.00-5.00
8" Virginia Gadroon plate................................$2.00-10.00

Chesterton (Teal)
This color is also called Corinthian and the ware is frequently backstamped Corinthian.

*9 pc. odd lot set...$10.00
*23 pc. odd lot set..$50.00
*36 pc. odd lot set.......................................$125.00-195.00
*Service for 12 ....$250.00
8 pc. Virginia Gadroon snack set......................$5.00-24.00
Cup & saucer set...$5.00-10.00
5" fruit dish..$1.00-5.00
6" plate $1.00-5.00
Lunch plate $2.00-8.00
8" Virginia plate $2.00-10.00
Dinner plate $2.00-10.00
Pickle plate...$2.00-6.00
*10" chop plate and lifter set...............................$10.00
Platters $5.00-20.00
Vegetable bowls..$2.00-11.00
7" shallow lugged dish $2.00-5.00
Flat soup dish..$4.00-6.00
Floral embossed Virginia cake set 15.00-35.00
   (13"cake/6 small plates)
Cake/pie lifter $5.00-20.00
Cream & Sugar set $5.00-20.00
Shakers set $2.00-6.00
Gravy jug $4.00-14.00

Chesterton (White)
See also White Chapel.

6" gold-edge plate..$1.00-5.00

Chesterton (Yellow)

10" lugged chop plate $2.00-13.00

Children's
Frogs & scarecrow child's plate $15.00-35.00
"Playmates" cylindrical baby dish $20.00-50.00
Doggy with blue & yellow lines
      child's dish and mug $20.00-43.00
Kiddo intaglio pink or blue mug $14.00-25.00
Blue duck with umbrella plate...........................$12.00-24.00
Blue octagonal hot water dish $19.00-50
*Complete Kiddo set, blue plate, bowl, mug..............$32.00
*Pink duck intaglio bowl.......................................$7.50
*Pink intaglio round hot water baby dish $40.00
*Bear/balloon blue intaglio kiddie plate $15.00

Chocolate brown
Used on Chesterton and Rockingham Reproductions.

Christmas Holly
(ca.1958) Harker name for unknown pattern.

Christmas Tree
(ca.1958) Harker name for unknown pattern.

Church plates
Usually unmarked. Round Gadroon blanks (glazed or unglazed undecorated) sold to jobbers who imprinted pictures of churches for fund-raising purposes.

Plate...$1.00-5.00

Clipper Ship
(ca.1937) Harker name for design on Embassy shape.

Cock O'Morn
(ca.1957) Harker name for intaglio design of rooster on coral engobe. The same design on yellow was called Rooster. Reportedly, this design was also used on pink and blue, but it is not documented.

Lunch plate $2.00-8.00
Olympic platter $4.00-14.00

Colonial Lady
Popular silhouette pattern from 1930's. Harker's used a lady from the 18th century and sometimes her suitor. The decorating department called this #7110, Old Print, or Silhouette.

*Virginia berry set (9" bowl/6 fruits)............................$25.00
Cup and saucer...$5.00-10.00
6" plate $2.00-8.00
8" Virginia dinner plate $2.00-12.00
9" embossed edge plate $3.00-15.00
Lugged soup/cereal $5.00-10.00
Vegetable bowl $3.00-15.00
Footed bowl $6.00-18.00
Casserole and spoon set....................................$12.00-25.00
Au gratin casserole..$15.00-30.00
Ohio paneled syrup jug.....................................$5.00-18.00
Modern Age syrup jug..$5.00-18.00
Arches batter jug $10.00-25.00

Color Ripple
(ca.1962) Harker name for Royal Gadroon with colored edge rather than plain white of earlier Chesterton.

Colorful Fruit
See Red Apple.

Concord
Lehner lists as a series. This could be the shape used for Stone China.

Coral/ Coral Sand
Used limitedly on Chesterton and frequently on intaglio. With tiny dark flecks, it was also a "fashion color" on White Clover and without flecks on Russel Wright clocks.

Corinne
My name for older pattern of black edge line with floral in pink, blue, lavender and green.

    7" flat soup $4.00-6.00

Corinthian
See Chesterton Teal.

Cornflower
(ca.1937) Harker name for design on Embassy shape.

Coronet
(ca.1957) Harker name for intaglio design of ring of leaves on gray engobe. The same design on blue was called Snow Leaf. I have pictured a plate with the design on celadon; I don't know its name.

    Lunch plate/green or blue $2.00-8.00

Cottage
See Doll House.

Country Charm
(ca.1960) Harker name for unknown intaglio design.

Country Cousins
(ca.1960) Harker name for intaglio design of birds in Pennsylvania Dutch style in celadon green or coral.

    One-tier tidbit..$3.00-6.00

Countryside
Cunningham's name for decal in curved perspective of cottage with garden and smoke rising from chimney.

    *Drip jar, no lid 18.00

Coupe
A generic term that simply means having no flat rim.

Crayon Apples
My name for pattern that looks like apples drawn with crayons.

    Batter Jug..$8.00-25.00

Cross Stitch
See Petit Point.

Curiosity Shop
(ca.1937) Harker name for pattern of a "shelf of gay tinted pottery."

Currier & Ives
(ca.1960) Series of decals used by many other potteries as well

    6" plate $1.00-12.00
    *8" Virginia Gadroon plate $2.00-15.00
    Dinner plate $3.00-24.00
    *Round Gadroon cake and lifter set with Violets $8.00
    *Round Gadroon cake plate/6 dessert plates......$18.00-65.00
    *Cake set with lifter $10.00
    Cake/Pie lifter $5.00-20.00
    *Sugar only..$6.50

Dainty Flower
(ca. 1930) Most popular name for the first intaglio design under Harker's Cameo backstamps.

    Experimental plate ....NFS
    Swirl cup $6.00-10.00
    *Swirl cup and saucer set $10.00
    *5" Swirl fruit dish.................................$.2.00-5.00
    5" Virginia fruit dish................................$2.00-5.00
    *6" Swirl plate $2.00-5.00
    6" Virginia plate $2.00-5.00
    7" Swirl lunch plate...............................$3.00-50.00
    *9" Swirl plate $8.00-10.00
    12" Virginia utility plate $5.00-50.00
    *Swirl platter $17.00-22.00
    8" Virginia vegetable bowl $10.00-20.00
    Zephyr cookie jar....................................$25.00-50.00
    *D'Ware oval shaker set $8.00-16.00
    *D'Ware oval jar with lid $12.00-55.00
    *Modern Age salt and pepper $10.00-17.00
    Skyscraper salt & pepper shakers.......................$3.00-15.00
    *Rolling Pin..$35.00-120.00
    *Zephyr au gratin set $10.00-30.00
    *Zephyr casserole.................................$10.00-40.00

*Set of 4 nested Zephyr bowls $25.00
Ashtray...$1.00-5.00
*Pie baker $10.00-30.00
*Custard $8.00
*Coffee pot $25.00-45.00
*Zephyr stackable with lid...............$10.00-15.00
*9" Zephyr mixing bowl $20.00-30.00
*Round jug and lid $15.00-45.00
*6" Ohio syrup jug and lid $13.00-30.00
*8" Ohio syrup jug and lid $13.00-30.0
*Batter jug..$28.00

Dainty Flower (Pink)

*9" Virginia plate $10.00-15.00
12" Virginia rectangular platter $5.00-20.00
*Gem creamer $20.00-30.00
*Zephyr teapot $25.00-50.00
*Skyscraper salt shaker only................$2.00-5.00
*Pie baker $10.00-25.00

Dainty Flower (Yellow)

Prices are often inflated because according to many sources, less was made than of blue or pink.

*12" Virginia utility plate...................$10.00-30.00
Round jug (no lid) $15.00-35.00
D'Ware shaker set $8.00-16.00
*D'Ware oval jar with lid $12.00-55.00
*Pie baker $60.00
*Rolling pin, plain yellow.........................$90.00

Dainty Flower (Teal)

Because Dainty Flower was not used to any great extent with teal, this is probably a true rarity.

D'Ware Shaker set $25.00

Daisy Lane

(ca.1957) Harker name for intaglio design of white daisies with turquoise centers on pink-cocoa. The same design was used on pink-cocoa with dark brown centers, but the name is lost.

Dawn Gray

(ca. 1960) A very pale gray used on Wood Song.

Deco Dahlia

(ca. 1935) The most frequently used name for decals in both blue and red with black, applied to Plymouth ware according to records of decorating department. The department called this Red Daisy.

*74-pc. dinnerware set $125.00
6" Virginia plate $1.00-5.00
*11" oval platter....................................$5.00
Range set (Skyscraper lard jar and shakers)........$15.00-35.00
*Skyscraper shaker set only.......................$22.00

Individual bean pot $3.00-8.00
Casserole and lid..............................$7.00-36.00
Utility bowl (mug) $4.00-12.00
Pie baker $5.00-25.00
Scoop...$6.00-45.00
Hi-rise jug $20.00-40.00

Delft

(ca.1940) Harker loved this name, I suppose, because it was synonymous for many consumers with china. This line was simply half plain blue engobe and half white. The only intaglio was "S" and "P" on the shakers.

*Fork only...$15.00
*Cake/pie lifter $16.00
*Skyscraper shakers $7.00
*Rolling pin $95.00

Delft

(ca.1960) Harker name for blue provincial decal on Stone China.

Delft Decal on Heritance shape

Lunch plate...................................$2.00-10.00

Diamonds

(ca.1960) Harker name for intaglio design of circle of diamond shapes on Stone China. Also called Kimberly.

Dixie

(ca. 1900) Older line of semi-porcelain. Flatware has scalloped edge, and hollow ware has paneled effect.

Dogwood

(ca.1955) Harker name for intaglio design on pink-cocoa.

Lunch plate $2.00-8.00

Doll House

(ca. 1935) Harker name for unknown decal. I wonder if it is the one researchers call Cottage or Honeymoon Cottage, a colorful simplified design of house with broad path narrowing as it approaches the door.

Donna

My name for pattern of pink and gray.

Cake plate and lifter set.................$20.00

Dresden

(ca.1940) Harker name for unknown pattern.

D'Ware
Oval hollow ware with "cap" effect used on shakers and jars.

Elk
My name for older decal.

Ewer..$65.00
Dresser tray $5.00-20.00

Embassy
(ca. 1930) Line with plain round flatware, coupe bowls. Hollow ware pieces have scrolled lugs, bullet-shaped finials, and D-ring handles.

Covered casserole & assorted plates $15.00

Enchantment
(ca.1960) Harker name for decal of blue and gray flowers on Shellridge shape.

English Countryside
Cunningham's name for a continuous decal design of a thatched cottage and a garden.

English Ivy
(ca.1939) Harker name for what looks like a buckeye leaf surrounded by small flowers in red, black and platinum on Bakerite, HotOven, and Modern Age marks.

Mixing bowl $5.00-40.00

Erica
My name for pattern of pink and gray flowers.

Oval lugged platter...................................$5.00-11.00

Etruria
(ca. 1900) Relatively plain amphora-shaped toilet set.

Eurasia
(ca. 1967) Stoneware line with stamped designs produced late in Harker history.

Everglades
(ca. 1957) Harker name for intaglio design of cattails on pink-cocoa also called Meadow Marsh when produced for Sears' Harmony House.

*15 pc. odd lot set.......................................$30.00
Dinner plate $2.00-10.00

Espresso
Listed by Lehner as part of the Concord series.

Fireplace
(ca. 1935) Harker name for decal in black and red of open fireplace with a teakettle over fire.

Flower Basket
(ca.1939) Harker name for decal of large flowers in a small basket in yellow, blue, brown, and red on Modern Age shape.

Forbidden Fruit
My name for an intaglio design on Stone China. See Lemon Tree.

Forest Flower
(ca.1960) Harker name for decal on Shellridge shape.

6" plate $1.00-5.00

Forever Yours
(ca.1960) Harker name for decal on Shellridge shape.

Fruit
(ca.1960) Harker name for decal of mixed fruit on Gadroon cake set.

Fruit on Amber
(ca.1960) Harker name for limited production intaglio design of a ring of bananas, peaches, and lemons.

Fruits
Cunningham's name for older decal of a branch of cherries.

Dinner plate $10.00-25.00

G.C.
Also GC. Actually an embellishment used on many shape lines. A series of raised parallel lines form a chevron.

Gadroon
(after 1940) Shape with rope-like trim at edges of flatware and as trim on hollow ware.

Game Birds
(ca.1960) Harker name for pheasants in flight.

6" round Gadroon ashtray.......................$2.00-6.00
Lunch plate $2.00-8.00

Garden Banquet
(ca.1960) Harker name for central floral pattern on Stone China.

Garden Trail
(ca.1960) Harker name for design on Shellridge shape.

Gargoyle
Because a tiny gargoyle trims the handle, this is used as another name for Regal jugs.

Gem
Harker name for sugar and creamer in HotOven line. It is a truncated cone with wing-like open handles.

Glacier White
Name used for off-white on Wood Song.

Gladiola
My name for older pattern of orange and blue glads.

 Mixing bowl $5.00-40.00

Godey
(ca.1959) Harker name for pattern of eighteenth century couples on Gadroon shape.

 *6" Round Gadroon dessert plates................................$25.00
 *6" gold-embellished Virginia cake plate $9.00
 10" lugged chop plate $2.00-13.00
 Spoon $5.00-20.00

Gold Diamonds
My name for older design of gold lines and diamond shapes on old shape.

 Cream and sugar set $25.00

Gold Clover
My name for older design of gold luster.

 *Luster trim covered dish...............................$65.00

Golden Dawn
Golden-yellow with dark flecks used on Stone China.

Golden Harvest
Listed by Lehner as part of Chesterton series.

Golden Spice
Used plain on intaglio and with flecks on White Clover.

Grapes on Teal
(late 1960's) Harker name for limited production line of double-dipped intaglio.

 9" experimental model ....NFS
 9" production model...........................$5.00-15.00.

Gray Hydrangeas
My name for old decal.

 *4 bone dishes..$36.00

Green blush
My name for practice of air-spraying green glaze on borders of designs.

 8" scalloped edge dinner plate with yellow rose..$3.00-10.00
 Dresser tray with pink roses $5.00-20.00
 Tumbler with pink roses $6.00-15.00

Green Rocaille
My name for older design of scrolls.

 Basin $35.00-65.00

Heritage
(ca.1960) Harker name for decal on Shellridge shape.

Heritance
Name used both for shape and for line. Plate has sixteen sides. Hollow ware paneled.

 6" saucer...$1.00-2.00
 5" fruit dish...$1.00-5.00
 Dinner plate $1.00-5.00
 Rosebud vegetable dish $2.00-5.00
 Divided vegetable dish............................$2.00-5.00

Hi-Rise
Also High-Rise. Shape name for tall, rectangular jug. Harker once called it simply "square jug," but later used the same designation for the Modern Age jug.

Holly and Berries
My name for older decal.

 Lunch plate $2.00-8.00

Hollyhock
(ca.1938) Harker name for unknown decal on Newport shape.

Homestead

(ca.1960) Harker name for decal on Stone China of a farm house and outbuildings.

Honey Brown

A mellow golden-brown used primarily on Wood Song and the Rockingham Reproductions.

Honeymoon Cottage

Most popular name for decal of house that looks like a child's drawing with wide path to door. See Doll House.

Hostess ware

(ca. 1935) Harker name for undocumented line that included Colonial Lady and numerous unnamed floral decals.

Iolanthe

(ca. 1900) A classic amphora-shaped toilet set decorated with medallions. Also used as a backstamp for the set.

Iris

Unknown pattern.

Italian Rose

(ca.1938) Harker name for unknown decal on Newport shape.

Ivy

Cunningham's name for green and rust decal.

```
Mixing bowl ............................................$5.00-40.00
```

Ivy

(ca.1957) Harker name for intaglio design on celadon green. Also called Ivy Wreath. When the edge was wiped to produce a wide white border, it was called Vine Lace. I have lumped all together here.

```
*8 place settings ..........................................$125.00
Cup ....................................................$1.00-5.00
5" fruit dish, plain or intaglio ....................$1.00-5.00
6" saucer, plain or intaglio ........................$1.00-2.00
6" plate, plain or intaglio..........................$1.00-5.00
Lunch plate ..........................................$2.00-8.00
Dinner plate .......................................$2.00-10.00
Plain oval soup ....................................$2.00-5.00
Olympic platter ..................................$4.00-14.00
Cream & sugar set...............................$5.00-20.00
Plain green divided vegetable dish.............$2.00-5.00
```

Ivy Vine

(ca.1949) Harker name (also called just Ivy) for classic green ivy decal on Gadroon or ovenware.

```
*6" plate ........................................................$5.00
Dinner plate .........................................$2.00-10.00
Gadroon teapot .....................................$20.00-30.00
Spoon ..................................................$5.00-20.00
Pie baker ..............................................$5.00-25.00
Round jug/lid ......................................$15.00-45.00
D'Ware jar/lid ......................................$10.00-22.00
```

Jessica

Cunningham's name for stylized floral decal.

```
Mixing bowl ........................................$5.00-40.00
```

Jewel Weed

My name for decal on Columbia ware that really looks more like morning glories; unfortunately, Harker used Morning Glory for another decal on Royal Gadroon.

```
Casserole and lid.....................................$7.00-36.00
Custard .................................................$2.00-10.00
```

Laurelton

(ca. 1955-65) A shape and line in which the rim of the flat-ware is embossed with a laurel wreath. Used as blank for Rockingham Reproductions plaques.

```
Cup & saucer .........................................$5.00-10.00
Lunch plate ...........................................$2.00-8.00
```

Leaf Swirl

(ca.1960) Harker name for decal of leaves in shades of brown on Shellridge shape.

Lemon Tree

(ca.1960) Harker name for intaglio design of tree with hand-applied yellow dots on white engobe (Stone China.) If the dots were gold, it was called Orange Tree. My plate, a gift from Paul Pinney, has blue dots. I have no idea what fruit it is supposed to be, so I call it Forbidden Fruit.

```
Dinner plate ..........................................$2.00-10.00
```

Lillian

My name for older decal of pink and gold flowers.

```
Dinner plate ..........................................$2.00-10.00
```

Lisa

Cunningham's name for stylized floral decal.

```
*8" Melrose plate ...........................................$5.00
Mixing bowl .........................................$5.00-40.00
Regal jug ..............................................$24.00-30.00
```

Lotus

Harker name for intaglio design of ancient Egyptian lotus blossoms on blue around edge of Heritance shape. Made for Sears under their Harmony House label.

Dinner plate $2.00-10.00

Lovelace

Harker name for a decal of a basket of fruit and flowers. One 6" plate with this design was marked "Ambrosia China" in gold block letters. I don't know if this was by another pottery or if it was another Harker stamp.

6" Virginia plate $1.00-5.00
12" Virginia utility platter.......................$8.00-40.00
*Cake lifter...$13.00

Magnolia

Harker called this decal Springtime, but because it looks like a magnolia and because there is also a Spring Time intaglio, I prefer to use this name, which Lehner used.

*Cup and saucer set $3.00
*5" fruit dish $1.00
*6" plate $1.00
*8" Virginia Gadroon plate $3.00
Dinner plate $2.00-10.00
*Vegetable dish $5.00

Mallow

(ca. 1940) The most popular name for decal of pastel florals and black accents on HotOven line.

*12" Virginia utility plate, lifter & spoon set.................$38.00
*Modern age cake plate.....................................$6.00
Mixing bowl $5.00-40.00
*Square refrigerator jar (marriage lid).........................$33.00
Paneled mixing bowl with lip...................$15.00-40.00
Custard $2.00-10.00
Coffee pot, no brewer $20.00-30.00
Syrup jug $5.00-18.00

Manila

(ca. 1900) Fancy scroll-trimmed toilet set.

Commode, marriage $40.00-60.00
Brush vase $6.00-25.00

Margaret Rose

(ca.1949) Harker name for unknown decal on Royal Gadroon.

Mary

My name for decal pattern in pink and gray. Valma Baxter

says that this was often called "Hal Harker's pattern."

12" Virginia utility plate $8.00-40.00

Meadow Green

Gray-green with tiny flecks used on White Clover.

Melrose

(ca. 1927) Squared shape with rounded corners and beaded edges.

Menlo

(ca. 1900) Fancy scroll-trimmed toilet set.

Miami

(ca. 1900) Fancy toilet set.

Miscellaneous Intaglio Patterns

Jumbo cup and saucer, "Dad"..............................$8.00-22.00
Jumbo cup, "Mother"...$5.00-14.00
Swirl "Pear" blue intaglio salad bowl $8.00-25.00
*Swirl "Tulip" blue intaglio salad bowl......................$8.00
*Swirl "Tulip" pink intaglio salad bowl $22.00
Octagonal Pearl Harbor trivet ....$3.00-$20.00
Octagonal "I Love America" trivet $5.00-20.00

Modern Age

(ca.1940) Narrow, oval body with finial like a life-saver. Usually, but not always had an impressed design of lines and *V*s like arrow fletchings.

Modern Tulip

(ca.1940) Harker name for decal on Modern Age shape.

6" plate $1.00-5.00
*11" Modern Age utility plate $6.00-15.00
Modern Age creamer, no lid $3.00-12.00
Modern Age teapot $15.00-30.00
Modern age cookie jar with lid..........................$18.00-45.00
Zephyr utility bowl $4.00-10.00
Pie baker $5.00-25.00
Custard $2.00-10.00
*Hi-rise jug...$30.00
Modern Age jug/lid..$14.00-35.00

Monterey

(ca.1938) Harker name for Mexican village design.

Lunch plate $2.00-8.00
Zephyr cheese tray $5.00-40.00
12" Virginia utility plate $8.00-40.00
Casserole/lid...$7.00-36.00
*Cake lifter...$18.00
Zephyr coffeepot with aluminum brewer $50.00
*8" syrup jug...$15.00

Morning Glory
(ca.1959) Harker name for unknown decal on Gadroon.

Mosaic
Harker name for abstract intaglio design. Also called Mosaic on Charcoal.

Moss Rose
(ca.1890) Transfer design finished in color by hand used by numerous potteries.

George S. Harker sugar bowl..............................$25.00-65.00

Nasturtium
(ca. 1935) My name for decal of yellow, red, and blue floral. This line was never stamped; logs of the decorating department specify "no stamp."

Skyscraper shaker set $2.00-26.00

Navajo
Harker name for American Indian design. This may be another name for Wampum, or they may be two separate designs.

Newport
(ca. 1937) Shape/line Hollow ware was spherical with life-saver handles and ball finials.

Cream and sugar set $5.00

Novelties
[NOTE: Like Advertising ware, novelties like this are priced according to subject, geographic area, and numerous intangibles.]

"Aspirations" plate $10.00-25.00
Betsy Ross plate $7.00-25.00
Dog on scalloped plate $10.00-25.00
*Eagle and Flag trivet.....................................$40.00
Gypsy portrait plate.......................................$28.00
Pastoral cows on Semi-Porcelain shape $15.00-35.00
Poppies inspirational plate $22.00-30.00
"What next?" Indian plate.....................$10.00-25.00

Oak Leaf
(ca.1959) Harker name for unknown pattern on Gadroon.

Old Carriages
My name for decals of carriages.
*Dinner plate...$10.00

Olympic
(ca. 1960) Coupe shape used for intaglio lines. Platters are rounded-off rectangles and cups look like half an hourglass.

Orange Blossoms
My name for decal of oranges and blossoms.

Cream and sugar set on Gem shape $15.00
Giant mixing bowl...$10.00-50.00

Orange Tree
See Lemon Tree

Orbit
(ca.1967) Harker name for stoneware with light and dark abstract circular pattern applied with stamps.

Oriental
My name for design on a pitcher. See Advertising.

Oriental Poppy
(ca.1942) This decal had a half-dozen names in its long service.

*8"x5" Melrose dish...$5.00
15" Melrose platter................................$12.00-25.00
Set of 2 nested Melrose bowls $2.00-18.00
Mixing bowl...$5.00-40.00
*Cheese bowl(Individual casserole)..............$15.00
Cake/pie lifter $5.00-20.00
*6 condiment jars/lids/rack $20.00
Florists' vase $15.00
High-rise jug...$20.00-40.00
*Regal jug $95.00

Pansy
(ca. 1935) Frequently confused with Mallow, this decal has pastel pansies with black accents.

*Casserole and lid $36.00
*Spoon $12.00

Papyrus
(ca. 1930) My name for abstract floral decal with Egyptian flavor on Melrose shape.

Dinner plate $2.00-10.00

Paris
(ca. 1927-35) Shape/line. I have not found any pictures or descriptions.

Parrot

My name for older decal.

Regal vase with multicolor blush.........................$25.00-30.00

Pastel Posies

My name for decals on Modern Age and HotOven lines.

Cheese bowl (Individual casserole)......................$5.00-15.00
Modern Age utility bowl...............................$4.00-12.00

Pastel Tulip

Most frequently used name for decal used by many other potteries as well.

Virginia dinner plate................................$2.00-10.00
Casserole/lid.......................................$7.00-36.00
*Skyscraper shaker set $23.00

Peaches

My name for older decal.

5" fruit dish..$1.00-5.00

Peacock Alley

(ca.1957) Harker name for intaglio design of peacocks on white Stone China. Also called just Peacock.

Cup & saucer $5.00-10.00
Dinner plate $2.00-10.00
Jug...$10.00-25.00

Peasant

(ca.1938) Harker name for unknown pattern on Newport shape.

Pepper White

Harker name for plain white engobe on Stone China. Tiny flecks of black metal chips inspired the name.

Persian Key

(ca.1966) My name for abstract intaglio on celadon.

Lunch plate $2.00-8.00
Dinner plate $2.00-10.00

Petit Fleurs

(ca.1959) Harker name for intaglio design of ring of posies on blue.

Cup $1.00-5.00
6" saucer...$1.00-2.00
Dinner plate $2.00-10.00
Oval soup/cereal bowl...............................$2.00-5.00

Petit Point

(ca. 1935) The name researchers usually use for a decal that looks like a cross-stitch floral. Often divided into Petit Point I (detailed), II (less detailed) and Petit Point Rose. The Harker decorators called all simply Cross Stitch.

Dinner plate $2.00-10.00
12" Virginia utility plate $8.00-40.00
*Virginia cake plate & lifter set $20.00
*Coupe oval vegetable bowl $10.00
Mixing bowl $5.00-40.00
Zephyr utility bowl $4.00-12.00
Individual bean pot $3.00-8.00
Casserole/lid.......................................$7.00-36.00
Fork $5.00-20.00
Spoon $5.00-20.00
*Fork and spoon set.................................$12.00-42.00
*D'Ware jar/no lid $18.00
*Skyscraper shaker set $26.00
*Modern Age salt shaker only $2.00
*Spherical creamer $11.00
*Spherical sugar/lid $16.00
Zephyr coffeepot (no brewer) $20.00-30.00
Octagonal trivet....................................$4.00-10.00
Rolling pin $25.00-120.00
*Round jug and lid $45.00
*6" syrup jug.......................................$18.00

Pheasants

My name for older signed decal.

Oval platter..$10.00-35.00

Pine Cone

(ca.1960) Harker name for monochrome cone and branch. From sales bulletin: "...truly a winner!"

6" plate $1.00-5.00

Pink-cocoa

A rose shade with overtones of beige used frequently on intaglio and less so on Chesterton.

Plymouth

(ca. 1935) I can find no photographs or descriptions of this shape name.

Poppy

(ca.1940) Harker name for pattern of poppies on Bakerite ware. Also referred to as Wild Poppies.

*Spoon only...$45.00

Primrose
Harker name for unknown Royal Gadroon pattern.

Provincial Tulip
(ca.1959) Harker name for Pennsylvania Dutch intaglio on celadon. Also called merely Provincial.

Cup & saucer $5.00-10.00
Olympic platter $4.00-14.00

Provincial Wreath
(ca.1960) Harker name for Pennsylvania Dutch decal on Stone China.

Dinner plate $2.00-10.00

Pumpkin
Lehner lists it under the Chesterton series. Probably another name for pink-cocoa or coral.

Puritan ware
(ca. 1935) Harker name for line that featured Amy I decal.

Quaker Maid
(ca. 1960) Backstamp name for line of cookware and tableware made for Pearl China and also under Harker name. Dipped in brown engobe and edged with "drip" effect. Sometimes called Rawhide.

5-pc. place setting.......................................$6-10.00
*Lunch plate $3.00
*Dinner plate...$3.00
14" salad bowl...$10.00
Individual bean pot $3.00-8.00
4" utility bowl..$4.00-12.00
Creamer..$2.00-8.00
Cream & sugar set.......................................$5.00-10.00
*Coffeepot, no back stamp............................$5.00

Queen Elizabeth II

Commemorative plate (1957)........................$25.00

Queen Mary
Name for unknown design.

Ragwort
My name for decal.

Cup..$1.00-5.00

Rawhide
See Quaker Maid.

Red Apple
(ca.1942) In 1949 brochure, Harker used the name Colorful Fruit, although in HotOven brochure, it was just labeled "10M." Cunningham names small continuous border Red Apple I and larger single decal Red Apple II.

*Complete waffle set (Platter and both jugs) $75.00
Jumbo saucer $2.00-5.00
6" Virginia plate $2.00-5.00
*Lunch plate $8.00
Dinner plate $2.00-10.00
*Scalloped edge dinner plate $15.00
Custard cup $2.00-10.00
Zephyr cheese plate $4.00-44.00
12" Virginia utility $8.00-40.00
*7" coupe soup bowl $8.00
Mixing bowl...$5.00-40.00
*Set of 2 nested bowls $4.00-10.00
4" Zephyr bowl $6.00-10.00
6" Zephyr bowl $6.00-10.00
Casserole and lid..$7.00-36.00
*Cake/pie lifter...$38.00
Spoon only..$8.00-45.00
*Spoon and stand..$13.00
*Fork and spoon $20-60
*D'Ware oval jar and lid $22.00
*D'Ware shaker set $23.00
Skyscraper drips jar....................................$12.00-18.00
Skyscraper salt shaker only $3.00-16.00
Modern age shaker set $22.00
*Modern Age salt or pepper only $1.00-5.00
Spherical sugar with lid $6.00-15.00
Zephyr teapot..$20.00-30.00
*Modern Age coffeepot $32.00
Batter jug, no lid $8.00-25.00

Red and Black Lines
This design is a dead-ringer for a line of Homer Laughlin. I suspect that it was shared out.

Teapot, Cameoware shape (squashed sphere).............$23.00
6" plate $1.00-5.00

Red Berry
See Blue Berry.

Red Doily
See Blue Doily.

Regal
(ca.1959) Harker name for unknown design on Gadroon. Also a shape name for pitchers with gargoyles on handle.

Regency Lovers
My name for an older decal that resembles a lithograph in shades of plum.

    Dinner plate $5.00-15.00

Republic
(ca. 1890) Shape decorated with many designs. The finials and handles were embossed with a small cross inside a circle. Carries both the George S. Harker crossed flags and the Harker Pottery Company embellished arrow marks.

    Scalloped white granite ware bowl $6.00-20.00
    Pastel roses shaving mug $30.00
    George S. Harker spoon rest.................................$5.00-25.00

Rocaille
(ca.1957) Harker name for intaglio pattern of scrolls on pink-cocoa. The name was also used at the turn of the century.

    Cup & saucer $5.00-10.00
    Dinner plate $2.00-10.00

Rockingham Originals (ca. 1840)

    Harker,Taylor hound-handled jug...................$550.00-600.00
    Benjamin Harker mug $50.00-100.00
    Harker, Thompson & Co. calling card.............................NFS
    Toby mug...$150.00-250.00
    Shell Spittoon $100.00-150.00

Rockingham Reproductions
(ca. 1960) Reproductions of original Rockingham items produced before 1860.

    Hound-handled mug $25.00-50.00
    *Green oval bread plate $35.00
    *White oval bread plate $17.00
    Honey brown soap dish.................................$20.00
    *11" American eagle plate $24.00
    *American eagle octagonal trivet $12.00-20.00
    6" American eagle plate....................................$8.00
    *8" American eagle ashtray...............................$20.00
    Jolly Roger toby mug
        honey brown or dark brown.................$5.00-25.00
    Jolly Roger toby mug, bottle green.....................$10.00-25.00
    *Hound-handled jug/6 mugs set $115.00
    *Green hound-handled mug $55.00
    Daniel Boone toby mug, dark brown..............$22.00-100.00
    Rebekah-at-the-well teapot $20.00-40.00

Rooster
Harker name for intaglio design of rooster on yellow engobe. See Cock O'Morn.

    One-tier tidbit..$3.00-6.00

    *Olympic platter.....................................$4.00-14.00

Rose
Harker name for intaglio rose complete with stem, leaves, and thorns on blue engobe. This is not Montgomery-Ward's White Rose.

    Olympic platter.....................................$4.00-14.00

Rose Minuet
(ca.1960) Harker name for unknown "rosebud center" pattern on Gadroon.

Rose Spray
Cunningham calls this an "all-over pattern ... made for the Harker girls." I have none in my collection. It is actually one of a series of patterns using the same decal, one that I call Shadow Rose. See Shadow Rose.

Rosebud
(ca.1959) Harker name for pattern on Gadroon.

    *Skyscraper shaker set $22.00
    Creamer only..$2.00-10.00

Rosemont
(ca.1937) I have no documentation.

Rosettes
See Shadow Rose.

Rossi Abstract
(ca.1955) Harker name for unknown pattern.

Royal Rose
Harker name for large deep red rose on Gadroon. See also Teal Rose and Rusty Rose.

Ruffled Tulip
See Tulip.

Rusty Rose
An undocumented name for a decal. In 1935 Harker used a decal of an orange rose with red-brown leaves. This decal (#7328, according to the decorating department) may be the Rusty Rose. See also Royal Rose and Teal Roses.

St. John's Wort
My name for decal that looks like that weed. On plain white Gadroon.

6" saucer $1.00-2.00
5" fruit dish...$1.00-5.00

Sea Fare

(ca.1957) Harker name for abstract design of fish on Stone China.

Covered soup bowl $10.00

Semi-Porcelain

(ca. 1900) Shape name used in Harker catalog for embossed scrolled ware.

Shadow Rose

Harker used this same decal in numerous ways on several shapes. It is a spray of roses in gold and pink with a "shadow" of gray blue. It is sometimes spaced around edge, centered, banded in ivory on white, and used other ways as well.

*Cup and saucer.....................................$9.00
5" fruit dish....................................$1.00-5.00
6" plate $1.00-5.00
Lunch plate $2.00-8.00
Dinner plate $2.00-10.00
*Virginia dinner plate....................................$10.00
*Platter $13.00
*Vegetable bowl.....................................$11.00
Royal Gadroon cream & sugar..............................$5.00-20.00
Flare open sugar bowl $3.00-7.00

Shell pink

Pink with dark flecks used on Stone China.

Shellridge

(ca.1959) Shape/line of semi-porcelain with shell-like striations along edges. Produced in plain white and with several decals.

Plain white gravy boat.........................$12.00-20.00

Shellware

(ca.1947) Swirl shape used primarily on Cameoware.

Sherwood Green

Name used for Bottle Green on Wood Song.

Skyscraper

Shape used for shakers and drip jars. As name implies, resembles classic skyscraper.

Slender Leaf

(ca. 1952) Harker name for design of stylized leaves in

browns on Aladdin shape.

Lugged plate in green...........................$2.00-10.00

Snow Leaf

Harker name for intaglio design of ring of leaves on pale blue engobe. See also Coronet.

Lunch plate $2.00-8.00

Souvenirs

[NOTE: Like advertising and novelty items, the price depends upon many factors.]

$250,000 Virginia Gadroon plate ....NFS
Attica, OH, with cherry branch..........................$3.00-18.00
Barcelona Lighthouse/Westfield, NY, plate..........$3.00-18.00
Brandon, VT, fish plate $3.00-18.00
Burlington, VT, elk decal plate $3.00-18.00
Cherokee, NC
        hand-painted plate on Va. Gadroon $2.00-10.00
Cincinnati, OH,letter-carriers convention $2.00-10.00
Conneaut Lake, OH, plate............................$3.00-18.00
Ft. Lauderdale, FL
        hand-painted plate on Va. Gadroon $2.00-10.00
Gettysburg, PA, plate, Godey on Va. Gadroon....$2.00-10.00
Lewistown, PA, deer plate.............................$3.00-18.00
Niagara Falls, NY, Indian decal plate $3.00-18.00
Ossining, NY, with strawberries $3.00-18.00
Park Rapids, MN, Indian maiden $3.00-18.00
Pittston, PA, Roses plate $2.00-10.00
San Juan, PR, postmaster's convention................$2.00-10.00
Sturgis, MI octagonal trivet..........................$9.00-15.00
Valley Forge, PA, Washington Memorial.............$2.00-10.00
Watkins Glen, NY, landscape plate $3.00-18.00

Spanish Gold

(ca. 1965) Harker name for limited production intaglio double dipped in gold and coral engobe.

Lunch plate...$2.00-25.00

Spring Meadow

(ca.1938) Harker name for design of small asterisk-like flowers on cookware in HotOven line.

Spring Time

(ca.1959) Harker name for intaglio design of flowers and grass in cocoa-pink engobe.

*23-pc. odd lot $29.00
Cup on blue engobe............................$1.00-5.00
*Lunch plate $3.00
*Dinner plate..$3.00
*Olympic platter.......................................$6.00
One-tier tidbit..$3.00-6.00
*Fruit dish...$3.00

Springtime
See Magnolia.

Star-Lite
(ca.1957) Harker name for stylized stars on light blue engobe.

Stone China
(ca. 1955) Line of ware made of gray stone china with pastel engobe. See also Peacock Alley, Sea Fare, Trinidad, and White Pepper.

    *Blue service for 4 ....$70.00
    Cup & saucer $3.00-5.00
    *Fruit dishes, 6 ....$8.00
    6" plate $1.00-2.00
    Dinner plate $2.00-8.00
    Platter $4.00-6.00
    Soup/cereal bowl.....................................$1.00-2.00
    Cream and sugar set $2.00-14.00
    3-tier tidbit tray $3.00-6.00
    Oil & vinegar cruets............................$5.00-10.00
    Cylindrical D'Ware shakers $5.00-10.00
    *Coffeepot...$12.00-30.00

Strawberries
(ca. 1949) Decal of dark strawberries. Embellished with gold designs.

    Dinner plate $2.00-8.00

Strawberries & Gold
My name for older design.

    Demitasse set...................................$125.00-200.00

Sun-Glo
(ca. 1957) Harker name for intaglio design of stylized sunburst on golden yellow engobe.

    Olympic dinner plate............................$2.00-10.00

Sweetheart Rose
(ca.1949) Harker name for Shadow Rose on Royal Gadroon.

    Cream & sugar set..$15.00

Sweet Pea
My name for decal of orange-pink sweet pea. The ware was apparently never stamped.

    *Rolling pin $24.00

Swirl
(ca. 1947) Shape used for Cameoware and other lines. See also Shellware.

Tahiti
(ca.1962) Harker name for line of gift and accessory items designed by Douglas Manning for "exotic Polynesian dining."

    *Olympic platter...$40.00
    Cylindrical ashtray $5.00
    Shaker set $8.00
    *3 pc. set: creamer/sugar/tray $10.00
    *Lidded jug $15.00-50.00

Tarrytown
(ca.1938) Harker name for "a modern design in gray and red" on Newport shape.

Tea for Two
(ca.1937) Harker name for decal of "whistling teapots."

Tea Leaf
It has been rumored that Harker under Columbia stamp made some of this old-fashioned line trimmed in copper-luster, but so far no one has documented it.

Teal Rose
(ca. 1952) Harker name for deep red rose on Alladin shape. See also Royal Rose and Rusty Rose.

    Dinner plate $2.00-10.00

Trinidad
(ca.1960) Harker name for design on Stone China of pastel flowers that look hand-painted.

    *4-piece place setting......................................$30.00

Tulip
Harker name for decal of shaggy tulip in orange-red and purple. Sometimes called Ruffled Tulip or Ragged Tulip.

    Pie baker $5.00-25.00
    Custard $2.00-10.00
    *Cylindrical stackable with lid......................$8.00
    *Skyscraper three-piece range set...............$35.00
    Syrup jug $5.00-18.00

Tulip Bouquet
(ca.1949) My name for decal of flowers with a large rose-pink tulip at center.

    Cake set with embellished edge
    (platter/lifter/plates)............................$24.00-50.00

Velvet
Lehner lists this under Concord series. I don't know if it is a color, a shape, or a decoration.

Viking
(ca.1957) Harker name for intaglio design of white diamonds on yellow Stone China.

Vine Lace
See Ivy.

Vintage
(ca.1947) Harker name for decal of grapes on Gadroon.

Lugged soup/cereal bowl.........................$2.00-5.00
Platter...$5.00-11.00
*Sugar bowl with lid $9.00

Violets
(ca.1959) Harker name for decal of violets on Gadroon.

Dinner plate $8.00-15.00

Wampum
See Navajo.

Wedding Bands
My name for design of gold bands on plain round white ware.

6" saucer...$1.00-2.00

Wedgwood Blue
Lehner lists under Chesterton.

Wheat
(ca.1961) Harker name for intaglio design of wheat made on pink-cocoa for Sears' Harmony House label.

Olympic platter.......................................$4.00-14.00

White Cap
Another name for White Pepper.

White Chapel
(ca.1960) Harker name for plain white Gadroon. Also sometimes called Puritan. The White Chapel mark was also used on other semi-vitreous dinnerware.

6" double-band trim plate $1.00-5.00
6" single-band trim plate $1.00-5.00

White Clover/Russel Wright Clocks
(ca.1951) Wright's first decorated dinnerware design. Intaglio clover on green, gold, coral, and charcoal.

Green cup $5.00
*Gold saucer (no clover)................................$2.00
*6" green plate (no clover)............................$3.00
*7" green plate (no clover)............................$3.00
Charcoal dinner plate $1.00-10.00
*Green dinner plate $15.00
*Coral tidbit (no clover)..............................$13.00
Green utility bowl.......................................$3.00
Gold salt & pepper shakers $5.00
Experimental design for ashtray $6.00
*Coral clock, no works $24.00
*Coral clock, original works $35.00-70.00
Gold clock, no works $24.00
*Gold clock, original works $48.00
*Green clock, original works $68.00

White Daisy
(ca.1959) Harker name for intaglio design of plain white daisies on yellow engobe.

White cup with yellow interior................$1.00-5.00
Olympic dinner plate.............................$2.00-10.00

White Rose
(ca. 1935) The Harker decorating department used this name for the Amy II decal.

White Rose
(ca. 1940) Harker name for intaglio design created under Carv-Kraft backstamp for Montgomery-Ward.

6" plate $1.00-5.00
Utility bowl..$4.00-12.00
*Cream and sugar, no lid................................$25.00

White Ware
(1879-1900's) Generic name for undecorated stone china and semi-porcelain produced at turn of century.

Dinner plate $3.00-10.00
Platter...$3.00-15.00
George S. Harker leaf dish $49.00
Fluted bowl $5.00-20.00

Wild Rice

(ca.1960) Harker name for intaglio design that had its own mark.

Custard $2.00-10.00

Wild Rose

(ca.1959) Harker name for decal of wild roses on Gadroon.

6" plate $2.00-5.00
Dinner plate $8.00-15.00
*Cake/pie lifter $5.00-20.00
*8-pc. cake set (with lifter) $25.00-35.00

Windmill

My name for older blue decal of windmill and canal.

Lunch plate $2.00-8.00

Windsor

(ca. 1930) Advertised in 1930, the first HotOven line was reportedly made on this shape, but I can find no pictures or descriptions.

Winter Asters

My name for old decal of pale lavender flowers on Semi-Porcelain shape.

Dinner plate $5.00-15.00

Wood Song

(ca.1960) Line of ware with embossed pattern of leaves, twigs, and seed pods. Finials and handles like twigs.

Tea cup & saucer..$5.00-10.00
Coffee mug..$3.00-5.00
Fruit dish $3.00-5.00
Butter dish...$5.00-8.00
Cream & sugar set...$10.00-15.00

Zephyr

Shape characterized by concentric circles of increasing size at the base of hollow ware that give a step-like effect. Finials are usually a sphere or a wing. Flatware also has concentric rings.

Schroeder's
ANTIQUES Price Guide

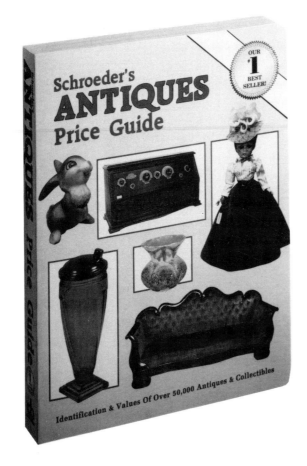

Schroeder's Antiques Price Guide is the #1 best-selling antiques & collectibles value guide on the market today, and here's why . . . More than 300 authors, well-known dealers, and top-notch collectors work together with our editors to bring you accurate information regarding pricing and identification. More than 45,000 items in almost 500 categories are listed along with hundreds of sharp original photos that illustrate not only the rare and unusual, but the common, popular collectibles as well. Each large close-up shot shows important details clearly. Every subject is represented with histories and background information, a feature not found in any of our competitors' publications. Our editors keep abreast of newly-developing trends, often adding several new categories a year as the need arises. If it merits the interest of today's collector, you'll find it in *Schroeder's*. And you can feel confident that the information we publish is up to date and accurate. Our advisors thoroughly check each category to spot inconsistencies, listings that may not be entirely reflective of market dealings, and lines too vague to be of merit. Only the best of the lot remains for publication. Without doubt, you'll find *Schroeder's Antiques Price Guide* the only one to buy for reliable information and values.

8½ x 11", 608 Pages   **$12.95**

COLLECTOR BOOKS
A Division of Schroeder Publishing Co., Inc.